REGIONAL DEVELOPMENT AND CONFLICT MANAGEMENT: A CASE FOR BRAZIL

Contributions to
Conflict Management, Peace Economics and Development Volume 8

SERIES EDITOR
MANAS CHATTERJI

BOOKS IN THE SERIES

Eurasia: A New Peace Agenda, edited by M. D. Intriligator

Cultural Differences between the Military and Parent Society in Democratic Countries, edited by G. Caforio

Managing Conflict in Economic Convergence of Regions in Greater Europe, edited by F. Carluer

Military Missions and Their Implications Reconsidered: The Aftermath of September 11th, edited by G. Caforio and G. Kuemmel

Conflict and Peace in South Asia, edited by M. Chatterji and B. M. Jain

War, Peace, and Security, edited by Jacques Fontanel and Manas Chatterji

Armed Forces and Conflict Resolution, edited by G. Caforio, G. Kümmel and B. Purkayastha

Regional Development and Conflict Management: A Case for Brazil, by Raphael Bar-El

European Defense Policy, by M. Foucault (Forthcoming)

Crisis Management and Regional Cooperation, by I. J. Azis (Forthcoming)

Peace Science: Theory, Methods and Cases, by P. Gangopadhyay and M. Chatterji (Forthcoming)

Arms Embargo Implementation—Comparing Experiences for Improving Effectiveness, by Michael Brzoska and George Lopez (Forthcoming)

Contributions to
CONFLICT MANAGEMENT, PEACE ECONOMICS
AND DEVELOPMENT VOLUME 8

REGIONAL DEVELOPMENT AND CONFLICT MANAGEMENT: A CASE FOR BRAZIL

RAPHAEL BAR-EL
Department of Public Policy and Administration,
Guilford Glazer School of Business and Management,
Ben-Gurion University of the Negev, Israel

Emerald

United Kingdom – North America – Japan
India – Malaysia – China

Emerald Group Publishing Limited
Howard House, Wagon Lane, Bingley BD16 1WA, UK

First edition 2008

Reprints and permission service
Contact: booksandseries@emeraldinsight.com

British Library Cataloguing in Publication Data
A catalogue record for this book is available from the British Library

ISBN: 978-1-84855-190-9
ISSN: 1572-8323 (Series)

CONTENTS

PART III: REGIONAL RESTRUCTURING – MACRO-REGIONAL POLICY

PART IV: SOLVING LOCAL FAILURES – MICRO-REGIONAL POLICY

PART V: POLICY RESULTS

LIST OF FIGURE

LIST OF TABLES

FOREWORD

The conflict between economic growth and balanced distribution of income is a well-known problem that has created tension, socio-economic pressure, hostility, and friction within many societies. The measures taken by many governments in order to improve the well-being of their citizens by promoting economic growth have led in many cases to satisfactory macroeconomic growth, but at the same time also to increasing socio-economic gaps and even to a relative deterioration in the well-being of significant parts of the population. Brazil is one of many examples of this phenomenon: in spite of economic growth the distribution of income has worsened for many years, and the poverty indicators are extremely high. Social conflicts nourished by this situation have been a major factor in the political upheaval leading to the election of a President from the Labor Party. Still, in spite of a clear "pro-poor" policy, poverty levels are extremely high.

The poorest states in Brazil are in the Northeastern region, one of them is the state of Ceara. This state has gone through a quite impressive economic growth in the last couple of decades. However, at the same time, the capital Fortaleza, once a quiet and secure city, has gone through a process of increasing social tension and increasing delinquency. Poverty rates are still extremely high (the majority of the population), and income gaps are enormous, between sectors of the population in the metropolitan center, and mostly between the population in the metropolis and that of the peripheral regions.

This book shows that this conflict between economic growth and the distribution of income, between economic and social achievement, or between the rich and the poor, cannot be solved solely by the means of transfer payments or other "pro-poor" policies. Such policies alone may help in the achievement of a better distribution in the short term, but may lead to a slower economic growth and to a worsened distribution in the longer term. Instead, the author argues that this conflict between growth and distribution may be attributed at least partly to the existence of a "spatial market failure." Such a failure is expressed by the inappropriate adaptation of demographic and social structures in peripheral regions to the needs of the macroeconomic growth. Identifying the elements of such market failure and devising a policy that treats them would therefore be the appropriate response to this conflict. Regional development as a policy for the resolution of this economic–social conflict relates to issues of spatial planning by the government, as well as issues of accessibility to production factors at the local level.

The case of the state of Ceara is used by the author in order to evaluate the existence of such a spatial market failure, and to derive appropriate policy measures. However, the most important contribution of this book is in the integration between academic research, policy evaluation, implementation, and evaluation. Since 2001 and until the end of this project in 2006, the Government of Ceara has fully cooperated with the research team: discussion of the diagnosis, decision about the appropriate policy measures, field implementation of policy, data collection for the follow-up and evaluation of results, discussion and adaptation of policy measures. This process was initiated by Governor Tasso Ribeiro Jeressati, continued by next Governors Beni Veras and Lucio Alcantara, and directed by Pedro Sisnando Leite then Secretary of Rural Development, with the active participation of all Secretaries, and mostly Monica Clark, Nunes Cavalcante, Carlos Matos Lima, and Alex Araujo.

The model of Ceara, as frequently called, cannot be copied by other states or countries. However, it certainly may be used as a model and adapted to needs in other places.

ACKNOWLEDGMENT

This study was sponsored by the Poverty Alleviation Project (Projeto São José) with the support of the World Bank and the Inter-American Institute of Cooperation on Agriculture (IICA). I wish to express my extreme gratitude to Dr. Pedro Sisnando Leite, the Secretary of Rural Development in the Government of Ceara, who provided this important opportunity to study the significant issue of rural poverty. I thank him for his valuable professional comments on all drafts of this book.

I also wish to acknowledge the support of the Governors of the State of Ceara: first Tasso Ribeiro Jereissati, who took an active part in the instigation and initiation of this study, followed by Beni Veras, and Lucio Alcantara who, with Vice-Governor Francisco de Queiroz Maia Junior, led the major effort of active implementation. I thank also all the Secretaries of the Government who took an active part in the analysis of the problem of poverty and economic growth in Ceara, and in the efforts to design the best appropriate policy model for this State: Monica Clark Nunes Cavalcante (Planning and Coordination), Carlos Matos Lima (Agriculture), Helio Barros (Science and Technology), Roberto Matoso (Labor and Entrepreneurship), and others. Last but not least, I wish to acknowledge the important contribution by Alex Araujo, Secretary of Local and Regional Development, who, together with his staff, took a major responsibility in the analysis, development, and implementation of the policy of the State.

INTRODUCTION

Economists and development experts around the world have recognized in the last decade that economic growth alone, as measured by the change of the gross domestic product, cannot be considered the main indicator for the level of development of a country. Probably more than anything else, the problems of persistent poverty and inequality in the process of economic growth has been major concerns.

Solving the problems of poverty and inequality by redistributing wealth (e.g., through taxes and transfer payments) may provide a direct solution to such a situation, but most researchers agree that this would be very short term. Such policy may lead to much smaller rates of economic growth, decreasing the potential for redistribution, and finally increasing the poverty levels to even higher levels. The huge challenge is therefore to find a policy that would improve the situation of poverty and inequality, while continuing a process of economic growth.

The State of Ceara, like the whole of Brazil and like many developing countries around the world, has been facing this challenge for many years. The problem of achieving the diminution of poverty and of inequality while achieving economic growth is quite complex and has been heavily investigated by many researchers around the world. The tendency of economic activities to be attracted to better infrastructure, labor force, and services, in many cases leads to the concentration of such activities in richer places, increasing economic gaps. While some researchers argue that a balancing effect occurs at a later phase (trickle-down effect, Kuznets U-curve), others suggest policies of public intervention for the diminution of inequality: adoption of compensatory measures (through transfer payments), sponsoring projects oriented toward specific population groups or sectors in need (such as agricultural development projects, support to the rural population), or supporting urbanization outside the metropolis. In most cases the free market has not actually led to a diffusion of economic growth to other places or sectors, and policy measures have not initiated any dynamic processes for the long-term solution of problems of poverty and inequality.

Another dimension of this complexity is that the reduction of poverty and the reduction of inequality are not necessarily positively correlated; you may achieve one at the expenses of the other.

Consequently, the required policy should be a comprehensive one, in an appropriately synchronized process, which includes urban spatial-restructuring together with the solution of failures of regional and local production factors. In this book, we identify this incoherence and derive necessary measures to overcome it. This differs from past practices in a few important aspects. First, our approach is not exclusively sectorally focused, such as rural development, nor is it pro-poor policy or urban development. Instead, it is a comprehensive approach, combining various dimensions of development. Second, it is oriented to the solution of market failures: public intervention should not necessarily focus directly on poor populations, but rather on changing conditions that could provide such populations with new opportunities, implying that not every rural place or agricultural activity, or every demographic group, should necessarily be supported directly.

A policy approach is derived from this diagnosis, expressed by public support of the adaptation of demographic and economic changes in regions outside the metropolis to the macroeconomic changes. Policy guidelines are elaborated at the local, regional, and national levels, and some specific initial policy measures are in a pilot phase of implementation. Based on the identification of main market failures, the first policy guideline is the support for regional spatial-restructuring and strengthening of a few identified secondary and tertiary urban centers, as a basis for the changing economic opportunities. The second guideline is the support of the development of new non-farm activities in those regions or economic sectors with growth potential. Policy measures include "reach-out" consultancy to remote small- and medium-scale enterprises, and support for technological development. The third policy guideline is the increase of rural productivity through public investment in education, infrastructures, regional organization, and agricultural development policy. Such measures, some of which have already been adopted and partly implemented by the Government of Ceara in the last few years, are apparently leading to a better urbanization process, leaving fewer excess labor force in rural areas and creating agglomeration economies at the regional level, which subsequently increase productivity and decrease poverty and inequality.

Many components of this policy are discussed in the book, and preliminary evaluations have been made. The results so far are quite encouraging. A spatial urban-restructuring of the area of the state has been performed, in view of the need for the development of regions in the interior

(4 secondary urban centers, 13 tertiary centers). A special ministry for regional development has been established and has installed regional offices for regional coordination and budget allocation. Nine regional councils have been established, including representatives of all sectors of the regional society, thereby increasing social regional participation and the improvement of "social capital" as a major input for regional development. Support for entrepreneurial activity in small- and medium-size activities has been provided to solve lack of access to public services.

Support for technological advancement is provided to improve the productivity level and therefore the income of small economic activities in the remote areas. A few pilot programs have been tested and are in a process of evaluation, such as a support program for tourism in the interior, or a consulting program to farmers in order to encourage them in the initiation of rural entrepreneurship projects.

It may be too soon to evaluate the broad effects of such a policy. However, the signs of change detected in the last few years look quite encouraging, and may be at least partly attributed to the effects of this policy. The share of urban population has significantly increased from 33% in 1960 to 67% in 1999 and 76% in 2004. The absolute number of the rural population is even decreasing. We find a decreasing rate of growth of the Metropolitan Region of Fortaleza (MRF) in the last years. The illiteracy rate has decreased in the rural area much more rapidly than in the urban area. The share of the interior in manufacturing activity has been constantly increasing. The share of agriculture in added value has increased, while its share in employment decreased. We also find an increase in the employment of the rural population in manufacturing. Increasing numbers of agriculture workers live in the urban area, thus increasing the options for additional employment in non-farm activities.

The results in the diminution of poverty and inequality are also quite encouraging. Most improvements in indicators that we find here are higher in Ceara than in the Northeast or in Brazil as a whole. We find a decreasing income gap between rural and urban labor force and a greater increase of income per capita compared with the Northeast and with Brazil as a whole. The Gini coefficient has been reduced. The poverty levels are continuously decreasing, and the level of income of the poor people is increasing in Ceara at a more rapid rate than in the Northeast or Brazil as a whole. The income gap between the richer and the poorer 20% of the population is constantly decreasing.

The intention of this book is to present the experience accumulated by the State of Ceara in the elaboration of a model for the achievement of economic growth together with the diminution of poverty and inequality as a basis for further discussion and for adaptation to other states. The model has already been presented and discussed in various professional international forums, and has received the support of highly ranked worldwide professionals.

The approach presented in this book is expected to show that the solution of poverty and inequality problems can be accomplished through the solution of market failures, transforming the poor people into active and productive workers who can contribute to global economic growth on a sustainable long-term basis using regional development.

PART I
PROBLEM AND DIAGNOSIS

CHAPTER 1

THE PROBLEM AND SOME THEORETICAL BACKGROUND☆

1. INTRODUCTION

We consider the well-known and painful problem of countries, mainly in the developing world, that suffer not only from low levels of economic development, but also from high levels of inequality and poverty. They struggle to solve their development problems by implementing various policies for economic growth (investing in infrastructures and education, providing incentives for capital investments, etc.), but in many cases it seems that economic growth, even when it is achieved, does not necessarily resolve the fundamental problems of poverty and unequal income distribution (Selowsky, 1981; Cardoso & Helwege, 1992).

The fact that national economic growth does not necessarily imply a diminution of poverty or inequality may be explained by the argument that economic growth involves a concentration of efforts in specific economic sectors or population groups, such as in the "big-push" theory (Rosenstein-Rodan, 1961). The diminution of inequality is expected to be achieved at a later stage, mostly as a result of a "trickle-down" effect. The "unbalanced growth" theory of Hirschman (1988) considers development as a chain of disequilibria – implementation of various investment strategies, the building of social capital, etc. Whether they are a direct consequence of national growth or are exogenously initiated, it seems that specific development measures are required in order to achieve a more equally distributed growth. The crucial question now is what those policy measures are, and to what extent they are actually efficient in the achievement of the ultimate goal of growth with a diminution of inequality. As will be shown later in some detail, there is a wide variety of policy approaches in this context. These

☆The first four chapters of this book and parts of other chapters heavily draw on a recently published article on this subject (Bar-El & Schwartz, 2006).

approaches include: focusing on solutions for the poorest populations, offering "pro-poor" interventions by supporting the poorest economic sectors, emphasizing the need for the attraction of foreign capital investment and the application of fiscal incentives for the redirection of such investments, and advocating the need for urban development in the rural areas. A broad picture of the various planning cultures in different countries is provided by Friedmann (2005) in an effort to identify a "global planning culture."

We do not deny the importance of the policy measures that have already been suggested as ways to achieve better distribution of economic growth, employment, and income. However, we claim that although many of these measures may achieve the direct objectives for which they were intended, they may not necessarily be the best instruments for the achievement of long-term national economic growth, and perhaps even not for the achievement of long-term diminution of inequality or poverty. Supporting the development of agriculture in a poor region may be counter-productive if such agriculture has no chance for a long-term competitive advantage. Supporting urbanization in a region may be counter-productive if it implies the inhibition of efforts of a nearby urban community to achieve agglomeration economies. Thinly spreading investments over too many projects in too many poor regions may ultimately be economically ineffective.

We argue that although inequality and poverty may not decrease simultaneously with national economic growth, medium- or long-term persistence of such inequality may be a consequence of a market failure when changing national economic structures are not met by the appropriate changing demographic and social structures in the national space. This is a market failure in the sense that certain physical and human infrastructures in various regions may not respond appropriately to the new economic structures, and the intervention of the state may therefore be able to create conditions for healthier development at both the local and national levels. In this case, it is imperative to first identify the specific components of the market failure, and then to devise a set of policy measures that provide the appropriate answers. The adaptation of such policy measures to the solution of market failures would lead not only to a compensating effect of the unbalanced growth, but more importantly to the integration and contribution of the poorer sectors to the national economy. For example, a detailed diagnosis identifying various crucial factors, such as the amount of excess labor force from agriculture, the potential for agricultural growth, the accessibility of the population to business services, the regional social structures, the regional institutions, and the potential for the development of non-farm activities, would enable the elaboration of a more efficient set of policy measures regarding the need for infrastructures, urban planning, support for agriculture, regional social organization, etc. A combination of such policy measures, if derived from identified market failures, would contribute to national economic growth and to a better spatial integration.

It should be noted that a conflict may exist between solutions for focused cases of inequality or poverty and the achievement of a global level of equality. Supporting agriculture in a given region may solve the problem of poverty in that region in the short run, but the alternative of supporting urban infrastructures for the development of industrial activities in a nearby town (and involving rural–urban migration) may be a better solution for the rural population in the longer term, and in terms of achieving a diminution of inter-regional inequality and contributing to the global national economy.

We shall next briefly review the question of the relation between growth and distribution, the regional perspective of this issue, and the policy approaches implemented as solutions, and then provide a general evaluation of such policies in the case of the State of Ceara in Brazil.

2. ECONOMIC GROWTH AND EQUALITY

The roots of this problem are to be found deep in the structural and complex processes of macroeconomic growth and its implications for distribution. The understanding of such processes may expedite the identification of policy measures that can facilitate the coexistence of growth and a diminution of inequality.

The issue of the relationship between economic growth and income distribution or poverty has been widely analyzed for several decades. Growth does not necessarily lead to a rise in equality: growth seldom occurs simultaneously across all people, places, and sectors. On the contrary, many writers have shown through various perspectives the potential of increasing inequality as a consequence of economic growth (e.g., Kim, 1997). In very general terms, the process of economic growth may require a higher concentration of stronger elements of the economy, for example, investments in regions with better infrastructures and populations with better education and skills. The "big-push" theory, first conceived decades ago by Rosenstein-Rodan (1961), implies concentration processes due to the indivisibility in production and in the supply of social overhead capital (among others). Such concentration processes naturally lead to the concentration in selected populations or regions of benefits from growth.

Another perspective is the potential conflict between achieving the goals of increasing employment and of increasing, income. Broadly speaking, achieving higher levels of growth and income generation may imply the adoption of higher technology or capital intensive processes, leading to a limited increase of employment (see empirical analyses, such as Morley (1978) and Bar-El (1984) for Brazil; Williams (1981) for Arkansas; and Jaksch (1974) for Columbia).

Economic growth is almost necessarily imbalanced, as suggested by Hirschman (1988), and this imbalance may itself have a provocative effect: Gains in some areas foster new demands that are responded to at a later time by economic activity in other areas. The hypothesis of the existence of a Kuznets U-curve (growth causes growing inequality at the first stage and growing equality at a second phase; see Kuznets, 1955), or of a "trickle-down" effect or a spread effect through which the first stage, inequality, is subsequently followed by benefits to the poorer segments of the population (growth first, distribution later) was not generally supported by empirical findings. To mention just a few empirical findings in the last few years, Michel (1991) finds a concentration of growth in higher income percentiles, and similar results using Gini coefficients, for the period after the 1982 recession. Lee and Townsend (1994) find comparable results for that same period in London, leading to growing gaps and a tendency toward long-term dependency. Limited trickle-down effects have also been found in developing countries such as Pakistan (Goheer, 1999), or India (Gupta, 2000), and Taiwan (Hsieh & Hsing, 2002). Recent theoretical explanations for the existence of a free market equilibrium at high levels of inequality have been elaborated, mostly on the basis of the financial market behavior. For example, Matsuyama (2000) describes a model in which the distribution of wealth in one period affects the supply and demand for credit, affecting again the distribution of wealth in the next period. Assuming that economic development projects that generate higher returns require a minimum level of investment, and assuming the existence of borrowing constraints, growth would lead to equilibrium with a growing inequality. Under certain conditions, however, the same model could lead in the long run to a Kuznets U-curve type of development, with a diminution of inequalities. Similar conclusions are reached using a model by Aghion and Bolton (1997), suggesting that government intervention may be needed for the achievement of decreasing inequalities.

The trade-off between growth and distribution should not be considered a static phenomenon that states a price to be paid in terms of social costs for the achievement of economic growth. The dynamic and very important element that is generally stated in most studies is the negative long-term influence of an unequal distribution on future growth. The argument in general terms is that a concentrated growth leads to the exclusion of a large proportion of production factors (workers, land, etc.) from the economic process, and therefore the prospects of growth are limited. An important model has recently been developed by Fishman and Simhon (2002), showing that a high concentration of wealth leads to low degrees of specialization and of productivity, and therefore to a vicious circle of under-development.

3. THE REGIONAL PERSPECTIVE

Following the main arguments presented above explaining the relationship between growth and inequality, we suggest that a distinction should be made between two patterns of inequalities induced by economic growth:

1. *Inter-personal inequalities*: These are caused by the concentration of benefits of growth in the hands of specific individuals who have higher levels of education, better access to finance, etc.
2. *Inter-regional inequalities*: These are caused by the concentration of economic growth in specific regions that benefit from better infrastructures, social capital, or any other advantages that attract economic activity.

For the purposes of this article, we shall focus mainly on the second pattern: inter-regional inequalities. If inequalities are at least to some extent the result of capital market or labor market imperfections, the question is whether an efficient free market equilibrium is reached through spatial concentration of economic activity (leading to inequality), or through a more dispersed distribution.

Industrial development has been used as a main engine for economic development in developing countries, absorbing excess labor force from agriculture, and leading to an urbanization process. We will not enter here in the polemics around the industrialization policies in developing countries and their influence on their development (see among many others, Rostow, 1960; Myrdal, 1968; Gwynne, 1986). Instead we will focus on the question of the influence of industrialization on the spatial features of urbanization.

Krugman (1991) established a significant starting point with the development of a rather simplified model for the explanation of geographical concentration of manufacturing. He explains, using a two regions/two sectors model, how a concentration of manufacturing activity may be found in one region, depending on the interaction among three main parameters: the share of manufacturing in the economy, the existence of economies of scale, and the level of transportation costs. This core-periphery (CP) model implies that economic efficiency considerations lead to a heavy concentration of the population around the manufacturing activity in one region (core), while the second region (periphery) will be less populated and based on agricultural activity. However, further developments of Krugman's model, mainly assuming changes in some basic assumptions, have led other scholars to different conclusions. Lanaspa and Sanz (2001) find that assuming the existence of congestion costs, and abandoning the assumption of constant transportation costs, lead (using the same basis of Krugman's CP model) to the existence of various asymmetric stable equilibria, thereby providing a "theoretical justification for economic landscapes in which large industrial belts coexist with smaller ones." We can state that the theoretical structure established by Krugman may justify a concentration of manufacturing activity, but, under different assumptions and parameters, may also explain a simultaneous growth in various regions. Krugman himself explains in a later article (Krugman, 1999) the action of "centrifugal" together with "centripetal" forces that may lead to the concentration of economic activity in more than one place. The coexistence of multiple locations of economic growth is justified by other factors in recent research: physical capital mobility (Forslid, 1999), the decreasing cost of trading ideas (Baldwin & Forslid, 2000), the differing qualities of land (Lanaspa & Sanz, 1999), and the influence of the public sector (Lanaspa, Pueyo, & Sanz, 2001; Bar-El & Parr, 2003a, 2003b). Challenging the CP model has led to the development of alternative models (Copus, 2001; Fishman & Simhon, 2002).

4. APPROACHES FOR THE ACHIEVEMENT OF EQUALITY

The problem of poverty and inequality is generally analyzed under three main perspectives. The first is poverty in rural areas, compared with the relative wealth in the urban areas. The second is the poverty and inequality within cities, mostly the larger ones, when part of the population enjoys a high level of income while the other part lives in poverty and unfavorable social conditions (e.g., the population of "favelas" in Latin American countries). The third is the inequality between regions, where some of the regions in a state (usually the metropolitan region) enjoy a relatively high average level of income and concentration of economic activity, while others, mostly described as peripheral, suffer from poverty and unemployment. All three perspectives of poverty and inequality may coexist in any given country: inequality between regions, within each region, and within each population group.

The major question is how to design a policy of economic development that will also achieve the objective of diminution of inequality and poverty, mainly in the developing countries. Some of the approaches that have been adopted in many countries sound very rational, but have not always achieved satisfactory results. We shall briefly mention some of them as shown in the most recent literature.

4.1. Helping the Poor People

One important approach is to provide direct help to the poorest people, in terms of remittances, welfare assistance, etc. This is certainly the most direct action for the solution of the problem for these people in need, but such an approach can be diagnosed as "non-developmental" (Ellerman, 2004). The results of such an approach are certainly efficient in terms of the alleviation of acute problems of poor populations, and therefore this policy should be continued, but it does not contribute much to the creation of a long-term process of diminution of poverty. Some influence may result from the increasing purchasing power of the poor or from their greater ability to join the labor force, but it is probably only marginal.

4.2. Helping the Poor Sectors

A second major approach is the provision of support to the poorest sectors – the agricultural sector or the rural sector. This may take the form of support for agricultural development (Dorward, Fan, Kydd, & Lofgren, 2004) or land reform (Balisacan & Fuwa, 2004). Another measure is "empowerment" of the rural population – better education and the increasing participation of poor people (Timmer, 2004; Berner & Benedict, 2005). Another policy measure is focusing assistance on rural skilled poor (Banik & Bhaumik, 2005), on young rural entrepreneurs (Burger, Mahadea, & O'Neill, 2004), or on other specific groups (Galster, Walker, Hayes, Boxall, & Johnson, 2004). Another version of this type of strategy is presented by Ellerman (2001) as the "rediscovery" of the Hirschmanian notion of unbalanced growth: looking for small "hidden rationalities" in small areas or in the periphery, and then helping these small beginnings to spread using the natural pressures of linkages. The general idea is to identify and support specific projects that are expected to yield good results and initiate a dynamic regional growth. Continuing in this vein, we can also understand the analysis made by Tendler (1989, 1993) of development projects in the context of the Brazilian Northeast.

Again, this approach certainly helps in the diminution of poverty and inequality (although it may also increase inequality within the region if the population assisted is the more educated and skilled one), but there is no assurance about the extent to which such measures are consistent with the country's macroeconomic policy. In fact, such a policy is based on hidden assumptions about the contribution of agriculture to economic growth, and about the population distribution between the rural and urban sectors. If the economic potential of the country requires greater focus on industrialization and urbanization, focusing on such a policy may even be counter-productive, by stimulating the "wrong" economic sector and slowing the urbanization process.

4.3. Attracting and De-concentrating Industrial Investments

A third important approach is the stimulation of economic activity by attracting foreign direct investments (FDI) and supporting industrial development (Hasan & Quibria, 2004). This approach is not oriented directly toward the poor population, but it assumes that the benefits of economic growth will "filter down" at some stage to the entire population through the increase in demand. The evidence of the existence of such a "trickle-down" effect has been questioned for many years, and was recently brought up again in relation to poverty alleviation (Mold, 2004).

It has also been shown that even where incentives achieve one economic goal, such as raising employment, they fail to secure the basic goal of creating competitive capability in priority regions. This is reflected in unchanged technical efficiency and the continuation of regional income disparities (Haddad & Hewings, 1999; Schalk & Unitiedt, 2000). Hence, these incentives often have no more than an ephemeral effect, eventually resulting in reduced employment levels in the long run (Cannon, 1980). Although it has been shown that incentives are of limited efficacy, countries continue to use them extensively, justifying this policy on the grounds that investments must be directed to weaker regions within the country (Oman, 2000).

4.4. Urbanization and the "Growth-Pole" Strategy

The same notion of imbalanced growth as described above in relation to Hirschman's approach lies behind the concept of the "growth-pole" strategy as conceived by Perroux (1955). Following the decreasing relative weight of agriculture in the process of economic growth, the growth pole is described primarily in terms of a complex of mutually related industries, stimulated by a specific leading industry (Parr, 1999a). Growth does not appear everywhere – it is concentrated in specific activities or places, and spreads to the whole economy. In a very detailed analysis that attempts to explain why this strategy was discredited, Parr (1999a, 1999b) discusses many neglected aspects, such as the spatial configuration of the poles, the economic activity at the poles, their external effects, and their embedding in the urban system. Among the most important conclusions derived from this analysis, he points to the necessity for a careful diagnosis of the regional problems and a clear articulation of attainable goals, a knowledge of the existing economy in the region, an appreciation of the existing and anticipated mechanisms for the transmission of growth at various levels, and an identification of available policy instruments, with interactions among all those elements.

Urbanization is a direct consequence of the process of economic growth in developing countries as a result of the changing economic structure: a diminution of the relative weight of agriculture and an increase of the relative weight of industry. This has taken the form of imbalanced growth, mostly concentrated in primate cities, as well as increasing CP gaps. As argued by Myrdal (1957), forces of circular and cumulative causation increase the gaps between central investment places and outer areas. Such forces may generate "backwash effects" (draining the periphery of its best production factors), unless these effects are balanced at a later stage by spread effects. The unbalanced development model as advocated by Hirschman (1988) actually implies massive investments in central locations, anticipating that the "trickle-down" effect will bring development benefits to the periphery. However, this strategy, like the "growth pole" strategy, did not lead to development in the rural areas of most developing countries. Rondinelli and Ruddle (1978) attribute this to the fact that appropriate spatial systems do not exist in developing countries. They devised a strategy of integrated urban–rural development, which considers the city as a functional element in space that should be adapted to the needs and potentials of the rural area. Rondinelli (1983) further outlines the rationale for creating large secondary towns as places for industrial development that provide markets and services to rural areas. This approach was later elaborated into a functional integration approach for the location of services and infrastructure needed for rural development (Rondinelli, 1990, 1993). Still, it remains to be decided which places are optimal for development as secondary towns, what kind of rural activities should be supported, what appropriate infrastructures are required, etc.

5. CONCLUSION: THE NEED FOR A RE-EVALUATION OF PAST POLICY

This short review of policy approaches for the diminution of poverty and inequality gives a broad picture of the variety of instruments that can be used by policy makers to achieve this goal. Each of these instruments is intended to respond to cases of inequality that have not responded appropriately to national trends of economic growth. However, this does not mean that the response of providing solutions to focused problems is the most efficient policy:

1. There is a need to integrate both the instruments to be used and the problems to be solved. As shown above, Rondinelli and Ruddle (1978) deal with the global problem of rural and urban development and consider comprehensive intervention policies. Friedmann (2005) also deals with endogenous growth, based on seven inter-related resource assets: human, social, cultural, intellectual, environmental, natural, and urban.
2. Intervention policies should be considered in terms of their contribution to the solution of market failures, and not just focus on identified problems. This would enable a healthier growth in the longer term, and a better integration of the national economy (in terms of space, economic structures, demographic groups, etc.).

The decision about adopting of a certain set of policy measures should not, therefore, be solely guided by the specific needs of a certain region or sector or population group. A diagnosis of the specific conditions should be elaborated at the global state level, with a distinction between regions and sectors. In addition, sets of policy measures should be derived as a function of specific problems as well as the market failures, in order to enable an optimal mix of equality and national economic growth.

The macroeconomic policy in the State of Ceara has generally dealt with all major elements of economic growth: investments in infrastructures, education programs, health care programs, employment generation, and urban growth. The result may be satisfactory economic growth, but occurring together with high poverty levels and gaps between the main urban center and the periphery (hereafter the "interior," as it is usually called in the State of Ceara). In other words, the macroeconomic policy may have been quite appropriate for the conditions of the urban metropolitan center that stands at the forefront of economic competition in the global context, but not necessarily for conditions of the interior, which require a basic structural change.

On the other hand, rural development policy tends to focus on the support of agricultural activities, an increase of productivity, the solution of land allocation problems, building of physical infrastructures, education, the stimulation of non-agricultural activities, and supply of production factors. Some programs in rural preventive health, creation of public works construction, agricultural extension, and public procurement for small firms have been analyzed by Tendler (1997) and found to be as successful. This may result in a significant improvement in agricultural productivity of the farmers reached by the programs. However, the increasing excess labor force from agriculture in the process of economic development (with the decreasing weight of agriculture) cannot find the necessary conditions in the interior for the development of non-farm activities that can compete with those in the metropolis.

An important potential source of increasing inequalities as a consequence of economic growth is therefore the incompatibility of structural economic changes and structural demographic spatial changes. Economic growth is mostly concentrated in and around the metropolitan center, while other regions, the "interior," may suffer from a degradation of their economic potential as a consequence of the decreasing weight of agricultural employment. Consequently, a major symptom of this is the increasing inter-regional inequality. The natural response of migration to the metropolitan center does not provide an appropriate solution for those regions, and creates well-known economic and social problems in the metropolis.

The lack of integration between the macroeconomy and the economy of the interior can therefore be considered a main core factor explaining the growing inequality. The economic transition of the interior from a mostly agricultural basis to a mostly non-farm basis requires the consideration of changes in structural policy.

A conceptual policy consideration should be related to the introduction of the interior as a basic policy unit, beyond the macro level and the local rural level, which may require specific policy measures. The prevailing policy concept has concentrated on a combination of macroeconomic and social measures, with focused treatment at the level of rural communities or of towns in the interior, with a few regional considerations. The problem of the interior is now much more than the aggregation of the problems of all its rural and local town problems. It should be considered as a whole sector of policy, as a segment of the global macroeconomic policy.

REFERENCES

Aghion, P., & Bolton, P. (1997). A theory of trickle-down growth and development. *Review of Economic Studies*, *64*, 151–172.

Baldwin, R. E., & Forslid, R. (2000). The core-periphery model and endogenous growth: Stabilizing and destabilizing integration. *Economica*, *67*, 307–324.

Balisacan, A. M., & Fuwa, N. (2004). Going beyond cross-country averages: Growth, inequality and poverty reduction in the Philippines. *World Development*, *32*(11), 1891–1907.

Banik, A., & Bhaumik, P. K. (2005). Supporting the poor but skilled artisans by making assets available to them: An empirical investigation in Rural India. *Journal of International Development*, *17*(1), 45–66.

Bar-El, R. (1984). Rural industrialization objectives: The income–employment conflict. *World Development*, *12*(2), 129–140.

Bar-El, R., & Parr, J. (2003a). From metropolis to metropolis-based region: The case of Tel-Aviv. *Urban Studies*, *40*(1), 113–125.

Bar-El, R., & Parr, J. (2003b). Over-reliance on the core-periphery model? The case of Israel. *Environment and Planning C*, *21*(3), 353–369.

Bar-El, R., & Schwartz, D. (2006). Regional development as a policy for growth with equity – the state of Ceara (Brazil) as a model. *Progress in Planning*, *65*(3), 125–200.

Berner, E., & Benedict, P. (2005). Left to their own devices? Community self-help between alternative development and neo-liberalism. *Community Development Journal*, *40*(1), 17–29.

Burger, L., Mahadea, D., & O'Neill, C. (2004). Perceptions of entrepreneurship as a career option in South Africa: An exploratory study among grade 12 learners. *South African Journal of Economic and Management Sciences*, *7*(2), 187–205.

Cannon, J. (1980). The impact of investment incentives on manufacturing change: The Georgian Bay region of Ontario. *Canadian Geographer*, *24*(2), 131–148.

Cardoso, E., & Helwege, A. (1992). Below the line: Poverty in Latin America. *World Development*, *20*(1), 19–37.

Copus, A. K. (2001). From core-periphery to polycentric development: Concepts and spatial and aspatial peripherality. *European Planning Studies*, *9*(4), 539–552.

Dorward, A., Fan, S., Kydd, J., & Lofgren, H. (2004). Institutions and policies for pro-poor agricultural growth. *Development Policy Review*, *22*(6), 611–622.

Ellerman, D. (2001). *Hirschmanian themes of social learning and change*. Policy Research Working Papers Series no. 2509. The World Bank.

Ellerman, D. (2004). Jane Jacobs on development. *Oxford Development Studies*, *32*(4), 507–521.

Fishman, A., & Simhon, A. (2002). The division of labor, inequality and growth. *Journal of Economic Growth*, *7*(2), 117–136.

Forslid, R. (1999). *Agglomeration with human and physical capital: An analytically solvable case*. Centre for Economic Policy Research Discussion Paper no. 2102.

Friedmann, J. (2005). Globalization and the emerging culture of planning. *Progress in Planning*, *64*(3), 177–234.

Galster, G., Walker, C., Hayes, C., Boxall, P., & Johnson, J. (2004). Measuring the impact of community development block grant spending on urban neighborhoods. *Housing Policy Debate*, *15*(4), 903–934.

Goheer, N. A. (1999). Poverty in Pakistan: Increasing incidence, chronic gender preponderance, and the plausibility of Grameen-type intermediation. *Pakistan Development Review*, *38*(4), 873–893.

Gupta, S. P. (2000). Trickle-down theory revisited: The role of employment and poverty. *Indian Journal of Labour Economics*, *43*(1), 25–34.

Gwynne, R. N. (1986). *Industrialization and urbanization in Latin America*. Baltimore, MD: The Johns Hopkins University Press.

Haddad, E. A., & Hewings, G. J. D. (1999). The short run regional effects of new investments and technological upgrade in the Brazilian automobile industry: An inter-regional computable general equilibrium analysis. *Oxford Development Studies*, *27*(3), 359–383.

Hasan, R., & Quibria, M. G. (2004). Industry matters for poverty: A critique of agricultural fundamentalism. *Kyklos*, *57*(2), 253–264.

Hirschman, A. O. (1988). *The strategy of economic development* [reprint of the 1961 edition]. Boulder, CO: Westview Press.

Hsieh, W., & Hsing, Y. (2002). Economic growth and social indicators: The case of Taiwan. *International Journal of Social Economics*, *29*(7–8), 518–525.

Jaksch, H. J. (1974). Income distribution as an objective in development planning. *De Economist*, *122*(1), 1–22.

Kim, K. S. (1997). Income distribution and poverty: An inter-regional comparison. *World Development*, *25*(11), 1909–1924.

Krugman, P. (1991). Increasing returns and economic geography. *Journal of Political Economy*, *91*, 483–499.

Krugman, P. (1999). The role of geography in development. *International Regional Science Review*, *22*(2), 142–161.

Kuznets, S. (1955). Economic growth and income inequality. *American Economic Review*, *45*(1), 1–28.

Lanaspa, L. F., Pueyo, F., & Sanz, F. (2001). The public sector and core-periphery models. *Urban Studies*, *38*(10), 1639–1649.

Lanaspa, L. F., & Sanz, F. (1999). Krugman's core-periphery model with heterogeneous quality of land. *Urban Studies*, *36*(3), 499–507.

Lanaspa, L. F., & Sanz, F. (2001). Multiple equilibria, stability, and asymmetries in Krugman's core-periphery model. *Papers in Regional Science*, *80*(4), 425–438.

Lee, P., & Townsend, P. (1994). A study of inequality, low incomes and unemployment in London, 1985-92. *International Labour Review*, *133*(5–6), 579–595.

Matsuyama, K. (2000). Endogenous inequality. *Review of Economic Studies*, *67*, 743–759.

Michel, R. C. (1991). Economic growth and income equality since the 1982 recession. *Journal of Policy Analysis and Management*, *10*(2), 181–203.

Mold, A. (2004). FDI and poverty reduction: A critical reappraisal of the arguments. *Region et Developpement*, *Special Issue 20*, 91–122.

Morley, S. A. (1978). Mudancas no Emprego e na Distribucao da Renda Durante o Milagre Brazileiro. *Pesquisa e Planejamento Economico*, *8*(2), 331–366.

Myrdal, G. (1957). *Rich lands and poor: The road to world prosperity*. New York, NY: Harper and Row.

Myrdal, G. (1968). Asian drama, an inquiry into the poverty of nations, II. In: *The industrialization issue* (pp. 1149–1205), New York, NY: Pantheon.

Oman, C. (2000). *Policy competition for foreign direct investment: A study of competition among governments to attract FDI*. Paris, France: Development Centre Studies, Development Centre of the OECD.

Parr, J. B. (1999a). Growth-pole strategies in regional economic planning: A retrospective view Part I. Origins and advocacy. *Urban Studies*, *36*(7), 1195–1215.

Parr, J. B. (1999b). Growth-pole strategies in regional economic planning: A retrospective view Part II. Implementation and outcome. *Urban Studies*, *36*(8), 1247–1268.

Perroux, F. (1955). Note sur la Notion de Pole de Croissance. *Economie Appliquée*, *8*, 307–320.

Rondinelli, D. A. (1983). *Secondary cities in developing countries: Policies for diffusing urbanization*. Thousand Oaks, CA: Sage Publications.

Rondinelli, D. A. (1990). Locational planning and regional economic development: Appropriate methods in developing countries. *International Regional Science Review*, *13*(3), 241–248.

Rondinelli, D. A. (1993). Location analysis and regional development: Summing up and moving on. *International Regional Science Review*, *15*(3), 325–340.

Rondinelli, D. A., & Ruddle, K. (1978). *Urbanization and rural development: A spatial policy for equitable growth*. New York, NY: Praeger Publishers.

Rosenstein-Rodan, P. N. (1961). Notes on the theory of the big push. In: H. S. Ellis (Ed.), *Economic development for Latin America*. New York, NY: St. Martin Press.

Rostow, W. W. (1960). *The stages of economic growth*. Cambridge, MA: Cambridge University Press.

Schalk, H. J., & Unitiedt, G. (2000). Regional investment incentives in Germany: Impacts on factor demand and growth. *Annals of Regional Science*, *34*, 173–195.

Selowsky, M. (1981). Income distribution, basic needs and trade-offs with growth: The case of semi-industrialized Latin American countries. *World Development*, *9*(1), 73–92.

Tendler, J. (1989). What ever happened to poverty alleviation? *World Development*, *17*(7), 1033–1044.

Tendler, J. (1993). *New lessons from old projects: The workings of rural development in Northeast Brazil*. Washington, DC: A World Bank Operations Evaluation Study.

Tendler, J. (1997). *Good government in the tropics*. Baltimore, MD: Johns Hopkins Studies in Development.

Timmer, C. P. (2004). The road to pro-poor growth: The Indonesian experience in regional perspective. *Bulletin of Indonesian Economic Studies*, *40*(2), 177–207.

Williams, D. G. (1981). Objective function trade-off curves in a rural economic development, activity analysis planning model. *The Annals of Regional Science*, *15*(3), 55–72.

CHAPTER 2

THE STATE OF CEARA: THE PROBLEM AND ITS ROOTS

The State of Ceara in Northeast Brazil presents a typical experience of macroeconomic growth at quite reasonable levels in the last couple of decades of the millennium, but with a too low impact on the diminution of poverty and reduction of inequality. In the year 2000, a decision was taken by the government of the state to analyze the prevailing development policy and try to devise an appropriate policy for the achievement of economic development together with a diminution of poverty and inequality. The data bases used here are therefore those that prevailed at that time, and were used for this analysis. The policy that was adopted by the government has been gradually implemented since 2001, first by Governor Tasso Jereissati, and later by succeeding governors, Beni Veras and Lucio Alcantara. Preliminary data for the period of the new millennium will be presented for analysis of results in later chapters.

1. GROWTH, POVERTY AND INEQUALITY IN CEARA BY THE END OF THE MILLENNIUM

The State of Ceara, located in Northeastern Brazil, is one of the poorest states, with a population of about eight million inhabitants. Its gross domestic product (GDP) per capita is less than half that of Brazil as a whole: it reached R$2,666 in 1998 (equal to about US$1,400), compared with R$5,560 in Brazil as a whole (equal to about US$2,900). However, the economic policy in the last decade has led to a rapid growth in the economy of Ceara in comparison with national economy. In real terms, the GDP of Brazil has grown by 34% from 1985 to 1998, while the GDP of Ceara has grown during this same period by 58%. Preliminary data for 1999 indicate an additional growth close to 3% and a growth of 5.8% in the first 6 months of 2000 (as compared with the first 6 months of 1999). This is a much higher growth than that of the whole of Brazil, which reached 3.8% in the same period. This has led to a considerable increase of this state's share in the national GDP, from 1.5% in 1990 to 2.1% in 1998, with a continuing trend till 2000. In terms of GDP per capita, the gap between Ceara and Brazil as a whole is still very large, although it decreased considerably during this period: the GDP per capita in Ceara was only 35% of Brazilian GDP per capita in 1990, and it grew to 48% in 1998.

Compared with the Northeast region as a whole, Ceara eradicated the 20% gap in GDP per capita within a decade, and now enjoys a slight advantage. The share of Ceara in the total Northeast economy has constantly increased, from about 12.5% at the end of the 1980s to about 16% at the end of the 1990s.

Still, according to evaluations by a World Bank state economic referendum, based on the Pesquisa sobre Padroes de Vida made in 1997 (Valdes, 1998), 55% of the rural households fall under the "high poverty line," and 17% fall under the "indigence line." There are a few alternative measures of poverty rates. We adopt here the measure used by IPEA (Instituto de Pesquisa Economica Aplicada) for the calculation of a time series of poverty rates. The poverty estimates are calculated from PNAD (Pesquisa Nacional por Amostra de Domicilios), an annual survey of the Brazilian Institute of Geography and Statistics (IBGE). The calculations performed by IPEA are based on a poverty line of R$68 per capita per month in 1999 prices (which is about the value of a minimum food basket, and roughly half a minimum salary). This is approximately equivalent to the measures used by the World Bank. The relatively rapid growth in GDP per capita was actually accompanied by a trend of decreasing poverty rates. The poverty rate for the whole state decreased from 73% in 1985 to 59% in 1999. While this high-level of poverty may be discussed further, as it depends on criteria definition, it is important to indicate that this poverty level did decline in the beginning of the 1990s, but has been stable since 1995.

An important and alarming finding is that, considering data for three population groups separately – the Metropolitan Region of Fortaleza (hereafter MRF), urban population outside this area, and rural population – we find large gaps between them and no clear indication for diminution of these gaps. There is no clear trend of diminution of poverty in the MRF, and poverty levels in the rural interior are much greater than urban interior, but the trend of diminution of poverty in the rural area is even slower (1.4% a year) than in the urban area (2.5%), leading to lower levels of poverty and at the same time to increasing levels of inequality.

Indicators of distribution do not show any clear improvement during this period. The most basic indicator, the Gini coefficient, as calculated by IPEA, does not show any diminution of inequality in the distribution of income in each of the three population groups. Other indicators, such as the share of poorest 20% or 50% in the total income, do not show any increasing equality. Furthermore, the ratio between the average income of the richest quintile of the population and that of the poorest quintile seems to be increasing during this period.

These high-levels of poverty and inequality coexist with the fact that the State of Ceara has achieved quite high rates of economic growth in the last few years in comparison with other states in the Northeast region and Brazil as a whole. A major reason for this is the fact that the majority of the population living in the interior of the country is still heavily dependent on agricultural employment, and is not fully affected by the state's economic growth. This leads to a situation where the economic gaps within the state are among the highest in Brazil. In fact, the existence of rapid economic growth in the state does not automatically imply a reduction in poverty. It is already widely recognized that the reduction of poverty requires the adoption of special policy measures beyond the ones that are required for economic growth.

The process of economic growth on a national-level is generally characterized by a few important patterns:

1. A change in the structure of the economy – mainly a diminution of the share of agriculture in the total state product and employment, an increase in the share of industrial activities, and at a later stage an increase in the sector of services.
2. A spatial redistribution of the population – mainly a decrease in the relative share of rural population and a parallel increase in urbanization, and a more balanced spatial distribution of the urban population; an increasing share of new urban centers and a decreasing share of the metropolis in the total urban population.
3. Increasing productivity of labor as measured by product per worker, resulting from changes in various factors such as an increase in capital intensity, a change in the economic structure favoring sectors with higher productivity, and an increase in factor productivity as a consequence of increasing educational levels and improvements in infrastructures.

2. DECREASING SHARE OF AGRICULTURE, BUT LOW EMPLOYMENT MOBILITY

The traditional economic basis of the interior has always been agriculture and cattle. The serious droughts that characterize most of the interior have always imposed serious problems on the economic growth potential of this region. However, a natural long-term trend of a relative decrease of agriculture in the economy has been strongly felt in the last decades, and adds other constraints on the development of the interior in addition to the drought problem.

The share of agriculture in an economy, mainly in terms of employment, naturally decreases with economic growth. Indeed, the share of agriculture (whenever we use the term "agriculture" in this article, we mean both crop growing and cattle raising) in the total employment in the State of Ceara did decrease quite rapidly, from 60% in 1970 to 44% in 1980, and to an extremely low-level of 35% in the drought year of 1998, but rose to 40% in 1999. However, this decrease in the share of agriculture in employment happened at a much slower rate than the decrease of its share in production, as can be seen for a few sample years between 1985 and 1999 in Table 1.

Statistical data about agricultural employment and production is very unstable, due to the changing climatic conditions in each year. The 4 years presented in Table 1 represent an average situation, and therefore can be

Table 1. Distribution of Employment and Product by Economic Sector in Selected Years (%).

	1985	1990	1995	1999
% in added value				
Agriculture	15	12	10	6
Industry	34	34	34	38
Services	51	54	56	56
Total	100	100	100	100
% in employment				
Agriculture	48	43	47	40
Industry	16	15	13	14
Services	36	43	40	46
Total	100	101	100	100

Source: IBGE, Pesquisa Nacional por Amostra de Domicilios (PNAD) (Various years) and IBGE, Annuario Estatistico do Ceara (Various years – 1998/1999, Table 11.5).

considered as representative of long-term trends. The table shows that the quite significant decrease in the share of agriculture in total employment does not yet represent the full picture of the decreasing share of agriculture in the economy: in 1985 agriculture provided 15% of the total product of Ceara, but its share fell drastically to 6% in 1999.

The gap between the rate of decrease of agriculture's share in employment and value added is the complete opposite of the expected gap in a healthy process of economic growth: we would expect a growth of productivity in a developing economy, an improving technology, and consequently a more rapid decrease of the share of agriculture in employment than its share in production. The data therefore strongly testify to the existence of a lack of adaptation of the agricultural sector to the process of economic growth in Ceara. A significant share of the excess labor force in agriculture does not find alternative employment in other sectors and remains in the agricultural sector, leading to low-productivity levels (as measured by added value per worker) and actually to disguised unemployment.

The economic growth of Ceara in the last decade has been led to a large extent by a growth in industrial activity. The preliminary data for the first 6 months of 2000 show a growth of 7.0% in industrial product as compared with 5.0% in Brazil. Actually, the share of industry in the GDP of Ceara did grow, but its share in employment remained quite stable, with a slight decreasing trend. This can indicate growing productivity in the industrial sector, but the ability of this sector to absorb excess production factors remained quite restricted. Its share in employment and product is still quite low. Instead, we see growth in the sector of services, mainly in terms of employment: the share of the services sector in employment, which was about 20% in the 1970s, grew to 40% in the 1980s, and stood at 46% at the end of the century. Some of this growth may be attributed by a rise in the demand for services resulting from economic growth, but it may again be a sign of an increase in disguised unemployment.

3. INCREASED URBANIZATION BUT A LACK OF ECONOMIC STRUCTURAL ADJUSTMENT

Independent of the drought problem, this natural trend imposes the need for a transition from agricultural activities to non-farm activities, a transition that may at least partly require a process of urbanization of the rural area, or migration to urban centers. This has actually taken place, and rural

Table 2. Rural and Urban Population Growth, 1940–1999.

Year	Population in Thousands			Population in %		
	Total	Rural	Urban	Total	% Rural	% Urban
1940	2,091	1,616	475	100	77	23
1950	2,695	2,016	680	100	75	25
1960	3,296	2,197	1,099	100	67	33
1970	4,362	2,582	1,780	100	59	41
1980	5,288	2,478	2,810	100	47	53
1991	6,367	2,205	4,162	100	37	63
1999	7,128	2,351	4,778	100	33	67

Source: IBGE, Censo Demografico (1940–1991); PNAD (1999).

population has constantly decreased over the years, from 77% in 1940 to 33% at the end of the century. As can be seen in Table 2, since 1970 the rural population has not increased at all (and has even decreased), while the entire population growth in the last 30 years actually occurred in the urban sector.

Referring again to the share of employment in agriculture, we find that the process of urbanization is faster than the process of creating non-agricultural employment. In 1999, 33% of the population lived in the rural area, while 40% were employed in agriculture, after a continuous decrease from 68% in 1970.

The process of urbanization that accompanies economic growth is generally linked to the process of industrialization: the decreasing relative importance of agriculture and increasing demand for industrial products leads to a concentration of population in urban locations. This is also true in the case of Ceara, but the empirical finding of a larger share of agricultural employment than the share of rural population apparently indicates that the urbanization process is not yet fully expressed by a process of change in the economic structures. Consequently, we are still finding a quite substantial population sector in the urban area that has not yet adjusted to non-agricultural activity.

4. INCREASED URBANIZATION, BUT WITH NO SPATIAL ADJUSTMENT

Urbanization is a natural response to the decreasing weight of agriculture but this does not mean urban concentration. Efficient economic growth is generally followed by the so-called rank distribution of urban population:

Table 3. Distribution of Population by Macro Regions, 1980–1996.

Macro Region	Absolute Numbers (thousands)			% of Total			Average Annual Growth
	1980	1991	1996	1980	1991	1996	1980–1996
1. Metropolitan region	1,580	2,307	2,583	29.9	36.2	37.9	3.1%
2. Litoral Oeste	545	640	674	10.3	10.1	9.9	1.3%
3. Sobral/Ibiapaba	574	639	681	10.9	10.0	10.0	1.1%
4. Sertão dos Inhamuns	365	373	383	6.9	5.9	5.6	0.3%
5. Sertão Central	527	535	530	10.0	8.4	7.8	0.0%
6. Baturité	177	190	199	3.3	3.0	2.9	0.8%
7. Litoral Leste/Jaguaribe	518	582	625	9.8	9.1	9.2	1.2%
8. Cariri/Centro Sul	1,003	1,101	1,135	19.0	17.3	16.7	0.8%
Total	5,288	6,367	6,810	100.0	100.0	100.0	1.6%

Source: IPLANCE, Anuario Estatistico (1985–1987, 1997).

the development of secondary urban places. The development of urban agglomerations is expected to provide necessary basis for economic development based on industrial and service activities. When greater levels of economic development are achieved, the rate of growth of metropolitan centers generally decreases (and in many developed countries actually equals zero or is negative), while secondary urban centers grow at a greater rate. This in fact did not happen in the case of Ceara. The picture of the demographic distribution by macroregions between 1980 and 1996 is shown in Table 3. In this table, the state is divided into eight major regions, where only the first one is considered the metropolitan region of Fortaleza, while all others are considered the periphery or interior.

The population of the metropolitan region of Fortaleza has grown at a much greater rate than any other region: 3.1% a year on average, while the next highest growth rate is much smaller – in the coastal regions at about 1.3%. Consequently, not only do we not see any process of spatial adjustment of the population, but also concentration of the population even rapidly increased during this time period. The share of the metropolitan region of Fortaleza, which in 1980 was 29.9% of the total population of the state, increased to 37.9% in 1996. The latest figures of the PNAD of 1999 show a continuing increase in the share of the metropolitan region, up to 39.0% (a population of 2.8 million out of a total of 7.1 million). The city of Fortaleza itself has a population of about 2 million people, more than 10 times than the next city in size, Juazero do Norte. The rapid growth of the metropolitan region leaves the interior of Ceara with insufficient urban

Table 4. Distribution of Economically Active Population by Economic Sector and Macro Regions in 2000.

Macro Regions	Agriculture	Industry	Services	Total
1. Metropolitana	5.4	53.4	54.3	41.0
2. Litoral Oeste	14.3	8.2	6.5	9.0
3. Sobral/Ibiapaba	16.4	8.4	7.8	10.2
4. Sertão dos Inhamuns	11.4	3.4	3.7	5.7
5. Sertão Central	14.5	4.4	5.2	7.5
6. Baturité	4.3	1.7	1.9	2.5
7. Litoral Leste/Jaguaribe	10.9	8.0	6.3	7.9
8. Cariri/Centro Sul	23.0	12.6	14.2	16.2
Total	100.0	100.0	100.0	100.0
Total absolute (thousands)	709	493	1,352	2,589

Source: Censo Demografico (2000). IBGE (Central Brazilian Bureau of Statistics).

bases for the appropriate development of economic activities needed to provide a solution for the decreasing agricultural basis.

This concentration of population in the metropolitan region of Fortaleza is further expressed by a strong concentration of economic activity, as can be seen in Table 4.

The data of the demographic census of 2000, show that most of the economic activity of the state in the growing sectors of industry and services are concentrated in the metropolitan region.

5. FACING ECONOMIC EXPOSURE IN A GLOBALIZATION REALITY

Together with the process of structural economic and demographic change, the interior also faces the trend of globalization and rapid technological development. The interior is not yet ready for exposure to competition in non-agricultural activities. Non-farm activities, mainly industrial activities and some services that produce tradable products (like commercial agriculture), are more exposed to external competition (unlike subsistence small-scale agriculture), and therefore can survive only if they are competitive. This is a reality that is new to most components of the economy of interior. The transition from a situation of an internally oriented economy, where a significant part of agricultural production and processed products are oriented to self-consumption or local markets, to a situation where most products have to compete in state or national markets, is extremely challenging. The globalization process exposes the interior to a much more cruel competition in the market and struggle in conditions, which were mostly unknown to its traditional economy.

The interior has not yet prepared itself with the required socio-economic infrastructures for entrance into the field of global competition. Non-farm activities require specific structures such as agglomeration conditions (urbanization), physical infrastructures, human capital, institution building, and supporting systems of finance and services, all of which are mostly lacking in the reality of the interior.

This situation is consequently reflected by a few symptoms, as are found in most developing countries. Several of them are indicated as follows:

1. Non-farm activities are few, and those that exist are mainly *those that are not exposed to external competition*: small enterprises, oriented to local markets.
2. The lack of appropriate urban structures leads to migration of excess labor force from agriculture *mostly to the MRF*. Rapid population growth in the MRF, with no parallel employment supply, leads to metropolitan gaps and poverty.
3. Revealed low-productivity in agriculture (product per worker), not only partly because of low-technology and business efficiency, but also the existence of disguised unemployment. The consequence is a low average level of income.
4. *Too small urban places* in the interior: insufficient conditions for the development of a competitive advantage and support of the rural economy.
5. *No economic integration* between the rural area and town.
6. A vicious circle leading to low expectations, low-levels of education, and low economic challenges.

6. CONSEQUENCE: TWO DIMENSIONS OF INCOME GAPS

6.1. A First Dimension: Rural–Urban Gaps in Ceara Compared with Other Regions

The direct result of the poor adaptation of the population of Ceara to the changing conditions of economic growth are shown by the data on average income levels in Tables 5 and 6. The data in Table 5 relate to the average

Table 5. Average Monthly Income and Gaps in Ceara, Northeast, Southeast, and Brazil, by Population Groups, 1999 ($R and Indicators).

	Average Monthly Income ($R) and Gaps				Persons in Ceara (thousands)	% of Total
	Ceara	Northeast	Southeast	Brazil		
All persons aged 10 and over						
Total	172	177	386	313	5,553	100
Rural	74	96	174	138	1,784	32
Urban	218	221	413	355	3,769	68
Gap indicators						
Ceara/others: total		0.97	0.45	0.55		
Ceara/others: rural		0.77	0.43	0.54		
Ceara/others: urban		0.99	0.53	0.61		
Rural/urban	0.34	0.43	0.42	0.39		
Economically active population (EAP)						out of 10+
Total	234	246	563	445	3,430	62
Rural	90	123	237	180	1,298	73
Urban	322	329	611	523	2,132	57
Gap indicators						
Ceara/others: total		0.95	0.42	0.53		
Ceara/others: rural		0.73	0.38	0.50		
Ceara/others: urban		0.98	0.53	0.62		
Rural/urban	0.28	0.37	0.39	0.34		
EAP with income						out of EAP
Total	314	334	667	552	2,532	74
Rural	149	197	334	275	781	60
Urban	387	404	706	615	1,751	82
Gap indicators						
Ceara/others: total		0.94	0.47	0.57		
Ceara/others: rural		0.76	0.45	0.54		
Ceara/others: urban		0.96	0.55	0.63		
Rural/urban	0.39	0.49	0.47	0.45		

Source: Calculations based on PNAD (1999, Table 4.4).

Table 6. Average Monthly Income in Ceara, by Population Groups, 1999 ($R and Indicators).

	Average Monthly Income ($R) and Gaps	Number of Persons (thousands)	% of Persons
All persons aged 10 and over			out of total
Total	172	5,553	100
MRF	258	2,222	40
Interior	115	3,331	60
Rural in interior	74	1,784	32
Urban in interior	162	1,547	28
Gap indicators			
Interior/MRF	0.44		
Rural/urban in interior	0.46		
Urban interior/MRF	0.63		
Rural/MRF	0.29		
EAP			out of 10+
Total	234	3,430	62
MRF	386	1,240	56
Interior	148	2,190	66
Rural in interior	90	1,298	73
Urban in interior	232	892	58
Gap indicators			
Interior/MRF	0.38		
Rural/urban in interior	0.39		
Urban interior/MRF	0.60		
Rural/MRF	0.23		
EAP with income			out of EAP
Total	314	2,532	74
MRF	459	1,027	83
Interior	215	1,505	69
Rural in interior	149	781	60
Urban in interior	286	724	81
Gap indicators			
Interior/MRF	0.47		
Rural/urban in interior	0.52		
Urban interior/MRF	0.62		
Rural/MRF	0.32		

Source: Calculations based on PNAD Ceara (1999, Table 4.4).

monthly income in 1999 in the rural and urban sectors of Ceara, compared with the Northeast, the rich region of Southeast, and Brazil as a whole.

The following are the main indications seen in this table:

1. If we begin by considering the last part of the table, indicating the average monthly income of the economically active population (EAP) who earn an income, we find that the rural–urban gap is greater in Ceara than other

regions. A worker who earns an income in the rural sector of Ceara receives only $R149 a month, compared to $R387 for the urban worker, a relation of 0.39. Much lower gaps (higher ratios between the rural and urban workers) are found in the Northeast (0.49), Southeast (0.47), and Brazil as a whole (0.45). We can see that the workers in both the urban and rural sectors earn much less in Ceara than Brazil as a whole, but the gap is much greater for the rural sector workers than urban sector.

2. If we now consider all the EAP (including those workers who earn an income and who do not because they are unemployed or because they work with no remuneration), the gaps are much greater, especially for the rural sector: the average income of all EAP in the rural sector is only 28% of the income in the urban sector. This increased gap reflects the existence of significant unemployment and disguised unemployment in the rural sector of Ceara, at higher rates than in other regions of Brazil. The data in the table show that only 60% of the EAP in the rural sector earn an income, compared with 82% in the urban sector.
3. Another indication of the existence of significant disguised unemployment is the share of rural population aged 10 and over that is considered economically active. It reaches 73% in the rural sector, compared with 57% in the urban sector. This probably indicates a strong distortion in the revealed economic behavior of the rural population: they, more than the urban population, tend to define themselves as workers, although they do not receive any income. Actually, the share of all the population of age 10 and over who earn an income is lower in the rural area (44%: 781,000 out of 1,784,000 persons), than in the urban area (46%: 1,751,000 out of 3,769,000).

The bottom line of the analysis of Table 5 is that for the whole population of persons aged 10 years and more, we can make two statements. One is that average income per person in Ceara reaches only 55% of that of the average person in Brazil as a whole. The second, the income gap between the rural and urban sectors is greater in Ceara than Brazil as a whole: the gap reaches 0.34 in Ceara (an average person in the rural area has an income of 34% of the average income in the urban area), in comparison with 0.39 in Brazil as a whole.

6.2. A Second Dimension: The Spatial Gaps

The rural–urban dimension represents only one aspect of the spatial gaps. One of the important consequences of a spatial disequilibrium is the existence of gaps between the metropolitan region and other regions, and between the metropolitan region and urban places in the interior.

An analysis of the internal income gaps on a spatial basis (the MRF compared with interior) combined with a sectoral basis (the rural compared with urban in the interior) is shown in Table 6. As explained above, we use here the term "interior" for all the population outside the metropolitan region. This population may be rural or urban.

The population of persons at the age of 10 or more is divided into 40% in the metropolitan region of Fortaleza and 60% interior, which is itself divided into 32% rural sector, and 28% urban sector of the interior.

Let us consider first the EAP that earns an income. We can see that the interior/MRF gap is less than the rural–urban gap: the workers in the interior on the average reach an income of 215$R a month, which is 47% of the average income in the metropolitan region. The fact that this gap is less than the rural–urban gap is that the interior also includes an urban sector, in which the average income is relatively high. The urban sector of the interior provides an average monthly income of 286$R, which is about double the average income of workers of the rural sector who actually earn an income. The existence of an urban sector in the interior therefore provides an opportunity for higher levels of income and for a diminution of the rural–urban gap. However, this role is not yet powerful enough: the level of income of workers in the urban sector of the interior is still only 62% of the income level at the MRF (see urban interior/MRF gap in Table 6). A further diminution of the spatial gap between the interior and metropolitan region therefore requires strengthening of the urban sector in the interior.

The biggest gap is the one between the rural interior and metropolitan region of Fortaleza. An average worker with an income in the rural area earns only one-third of the income of the same worker in the MRF: 149$R, compared with 459$R. The gap is even greater when we consider the fact that only a relatively small proportion of the rural workers earn an income: 60%, compared to 83% in the MRF and 81% in urban sector of the interior. This results in even greater gaps when we consider the entire population aged 10 and older, as can be seen in Table 6.

7. CONSEQUENCE: ECONOMIC STRUCTURE

The low-levels of income in Ceara, and especially in the rural sector, reflect both a distribution of employment with a relatively high representation of branches with low-productivity and income, and a lower productivity for each given economic branch. We shall first examine the distribution of economic sectors in Ceara in comparison with other regions, and later income level within each sector.

7.1. Distribution of Economic Branches

The distribution of employment between the economic branches is presented in Table 7. It includes all workers aged 10 or above, whether or not they receive an income.

As shown above, both the share of agriculture in total employment and rural population in total population decrease as a result of economic growth. We indicated above that the decrease of the share of agricultural employment did not follow the decrease of the share of agricultural production, leading to a probable disguised unemployment and low-productivity. The data in Table 7 actually show that the share of agriculture in employment in Ceara is still very high, in comparison to Brazil as a whole, and certainly in comparison to richer regions such as the Southeast. Forty percent of employment in Ceara is still in the agricultural sector, similar to that of the Northeast, but it is much greater than the share of agriculture in employment in all of Brazil (24%) and the Southeast (13%).

Table 7. Distribution of Employed Workers Aged 10 and More by Sector of Main Economic Activity and by Region, 1999.

Economic Sector	Ceara (%)	Northeast (%)	Southeast (%)	Brazil (%)
Total	100	100	97	100
Agriculture	40	41	13	24
Manufacturing	9	7	14	12
Construction	5	6	7	7
Other industry	0	1	1	1
Commerce	13	12	14	13
Services	17	15	22	19
Economic services	2	2	5	4
Transportation and communication	2	3	5	4
Social services	8	8	10	9
Public administration	3	4	4	5
Others	1	1	2	2

Source: Elaboration of data from PNAD (1999, Table 4.28).

Table 8. Share of Agriculture in Employment and Share of Rural Population, by Region, 1999.

	Ceara	Northeast	Southeast	Brazil
% of agriculture in employment	40	41	13	24
% of rural population	33	36	11	20

Source: Elaboration of data from PNAD (1999, Tables 4.28, 1.1).

Manufacturing is expected to be a major leader in economic development, but it reaches only 9% in Ceara, compared with much higher rates in other regions. Low-levels of employment are also found in important leading economic branches such as services for the economic activity, transportation, and communication.

In sum, the economic structure of Ceara's economy is still characteristic of a quite low-level of development. Such a high share of employment in agriculture is not consistent with efforts to decrease poverty levels, and improve income and standards of living. This is also directly linked to the inappropriate level of urbanization. The development of non-agricultural activities is generally related to a higher level of urbanization, and both processes – industrialization and urbanization – should be considered simultaneously. As can be seen in Table 8, comparing Ceara and other regions, there is a quite strong relationship between the share of agriculture in employment and rural population.

7.2. Low-Productivity in Each Economic Branch

Poverty and low-income levels result not only from the existence of a too poor economic structure, but also from a low-level of productivity in each economic branch, as represented by the level of salary per worker. A comparison of Ceara and other regions in relation to the level of income, as measured by the share of workers who receive a salary that is not greater than a minimum salary and workers who receive no income at all is presented in Table 9. Column (1) for each region shows the share of occupied workers with an income of one minimum salary or less, out of the entire resident population that receives remuneration. For the total of Ceara, we find that half the workers who receive a salary receive one minimum salary or less: this is double the average number of workers in Brazil as a whole. In addition to these, an extremely high share of 25% of all

Table 9. Income Levels in Main Economic Activity by Economic Sector and by Region, 1999.

Economic Sector	Ceara (1)	Ceara (2)	Northeast (1)	Northeast (2)	Southeast (1)	Southeast (2)	Brazil (1)	Brazil (2)	Ceara/Brazil (1)	Ceara/Brazil (2)
Total	50	25	48	24	14	8	24	14	2.07	1.74
Agriculture	76	54	68	51	32	38	48	47	1.59	1.14
Manufacturing	45	4	36	7	7	2	13	3	3.55	1.29
Construction	27	3	40	4	8	3	17	4	1.60	0.84
Other industry	48	1	34	3	10	0	17	1	2.82	1.09
Commerce	34	15	37	14	13	5	20	9	1.66	1.73
Services	62	7	59	6	25	3	36	4	1.71	1.64
Economic services	18	3	21	2	7	1	10	2	1.88	2.11
Transportation, communication	23	2	23	2	4	1	9	1	2.69	1.84
Social services	39	2	32	2	7	2	15	2	2.65	0.72
Public administration	25	0	28	1	5	0	13	0	1.97	0.44
Others	37	1	38	1	6	1	15	1	2.45	0.60

(1) % of Occupied Workers with up to one Minimum Salary, of Total Occupied Workers with an Income.
(2) % of unpaid occupied workers of total occupied workers

Source: Elaboration of data from PNAD (1999, Table 4.28).

workers in Ceara do not receive any remuneration at all, compared to 14% in Brazil as a whole, as shown in column (2). If we consider the Southeast region as representing some kind of potential optimum for Ceara, we find extremely high-gaps in income. Although the situation in Ceara is not much different from that of the Northeast as a whole, these gaps are quite significant and indicate the existence of low-labor productivity, and a large potential for development.

The analysis by economic sector shows that the productivity gaps should not be attributed only to the prevalence of an agricultural economy in Ceara. For each economic sector, we find much lower levels of income in Ceara than Brazil as a whole. The agricultural sector provides lower incomes than any other sector all over the country. Even in the quite rich region of the Southeast, we find that 38% of the workers in agriculture do not receive remuneration, and among those who are remunerated, a third are paid one minimum salary or less. However, the situation in Ceara is much worse: 54% do not receive any remuneration, and among those who are remunerated, 76% do not get paid more than one minimum salary. This certainly calls for a vigorous improvement of the agricultural sector in Ceara.

Probably even more alarming finding is the situation in the manufacturing sector (as well as in other non-agricultural sectors), which is expected to serve as an instrument for the solution of the problems of poverty and economic development in Ceara. The gap between Ceara and Brazil as a whole is much greater for manufacturing than agriculture. The share of remunerated workers who do not exceed one minimum salary is 3.55 times greater in Ceara than Brazil as a whole. The gaps with the Southeast are naturally much larger. A similar picture of all other economic branches is revealed in the table.

8. CONCLUSION: A GENERAL DIAGNOSIS – THE STARTING POINT FOR THE CONSIDERATION OF A NEW POLICY

The State of Ceara has in the last decade experienced quite an impressive economic growth. The GDP and GDP per capita have grown more rapidly than the Brazilian average, and therefore the economy of Ceara is now taking a more important share of the economy of the Northeast and total Brazilian economy. However, in spite of this encouraging economic growth, the State of Ceara is experiencing one of the greatest levels of poverty in the country, as well as unacceptable gaps between the rural and urban sectors, between the metropolitan region of Fortaleza and interior, and within rural sector. It is therefore of extreme importance to understand the roots of this problem in order to adept the public policy to the needs of the population of Ceara.

We should state that the existence of a process of economic growth at the level of the state is not necessarily expected to lead to a diminution of poverty or reduction of economic gaps. On the contrary, many ingredients in the process of economic growth may have a polarizing effect. Economic growth is usually led by the stronger elements of the economy – regions with better infrastructures, populations with higher levels of education, or professional skills, etc. The conviction generally accepted today is that growth is a necessary, but not sufficient, condition for the eradication of poverty. It is a prerequisite because it helps provide necessary public goods, such as education, health services, and infrastructures and brings an increase in the creation of jobs. However, it has also been claimed that growth is not even necessary for the reduction of poverty (Jentsch, 2000): poverty should be directly treated by the promotion of structural reforms and improvement of framework conditions in favor of the poor.

In any case, it is clear that the achievement of a more balanced economic growth, accompanied by a more equal distribution of income and a reduction of poverty, requires the adoption of appropriate specific public policy measures. Such measures are expected to play a part in the achievement of a more equal economic growth, and mainly to provide a stronger basis for long-term stable economic growth.

Effective economic growth is generally accompanied by the processes of industrialization and urbanization. Optimally, the improving productivity in agriculture within the process of economic growth, together with an increasing relative demand for industrial products, is expected to lead to lower shares of agricultural employment, higher shares of industry, and a process of urbanization. This process of urbanization is also expected to initiate a decentralization trend, with the development of urban centers in the periphery in addition to the primate city. The analysis of the situation in Ceara leads to the following evaluations:

1. *Urbanization*: A continuous process of urbanization has actually occurred during the last few decades. However, the economic growth of Ceara has mainly affected the metropolitan region of Fortaleza and to a much lesser extent the interior of the state. The share of the metropolitan region has grown constantly, both in terms of population and economic activities. This may be a natural response to the potentials of economic growth, since the metropolitan region is better equipped

than interior for the development of more advanced economic activities. However, such a process leads to social and economic inequalities in the short-run and economic inefficiencies in development in the long-run. This polarization process leads to a decreasing ability of the interior to develop a competitive advantage over the metropolitan region, and therefore to a waste of the potential of human and natural resources. Policy measures should therefore be considered in order to add a decentralization element to the process of urbanization.

2. *Changing economic structure – industrialization*: The natural process of a decreasing share of agriculture and an increasing share of industry has taken place in Ceara, as expected in an economic development process, but not in an optimal way. First, the industrialization potential has not actually been entirely achieved. The share of industrial employment did grow, but is still quite low. The productivity of industrial activity is low, and the income it provides to the industrial workers is much lower than the average industrial income in Brazil, leaving many of them under the poverty line. This may be attributed to the lack of appropriate conditions for attracting more productive industrial activities: lack of urban infrastructures – at least in the interior, low-levels of education and professional skills, low-technological levels, inappropriate organizational structures, etc. Limited availability of jobs in industry and low-levels of industrial productivity, together with expectations that this situation will continue, inhibit the effective absorption of excess labor force from agriculture, and limit the provision of a solution to the poverty problem. The achievement of higher levels of industrial employment and productivity is essential for the diminution of poverty, and requires policy measures that can stimulate the establishment of industrial activities of higher technological levels and with higher competitive ability.
3. *Changing economic structure – decreasing share of agriculture*: The decreasing share of agriculture in the economy of Ceara does not reflect a healthy process of improving technology and productivity and natural shifting of employment to other economic branches. The share of agricultural product in the GDP of Ceara has probably decreased too rapidly and agricultural employment out of total employment has probably decreased too slowly. A more efficient agricultural development could lead to moderate rate of decrease in the share of agriculture in total production. The "Rumo ao Desenvolvimento Rural do Ceara" (see IPLANCE, Governo do Estado do Ceara, 1999) published by the Secretariat of Rural Development sets an annual growth of 3–5% of agricultural production as an objective. This may be a quite ambitious

target, but it could be feasible in case the total economic growth of the economy achieves higher rates. Most alarming is the slow rate of decrease in the share of agriculture in employment. First, this reflects the too slow technological progress in agriculture, leading to still high labor intensity. Second, it reflects the shortage of alternative employment in other economic branches, leading the rural population to remain in the agricultural sector, and actually creating disguised unemployment. All this is reflected by the extremely low-levels of income in this sector, compared with Brazil as a whole and even the Northeast region. The diminution of poverty and creation of a healthy process of economic development therefore require the improvement of agricultural productivity, as much as for non-agricultural activities.

The combination of a reasonable macroeconomic growth with persistent levels of inequality and poverty led the government of Ceara in 2000 to the realization of a need for the reevaluation of their traditional economic development policy. Our diagnosis shows that high poverty levels in Ceara, in spite of a rapid economic growth in the last decade, can be seen as a consequence of combined imbalances in the spatial and economic structures. The concentration of economic growth in the metropolitan region of Fortaleza has deprived the interior regions of the chance to achieve their development potential. The process of industrialization is not supported in the interior by the existence of appropriate urban amenities, and therefore is not strong enough to attract the labor force from the rural sector. On the other hand, the relative demand for the output from the agricultural sector decreases constantly, its productivity level is still low, and still provides a poor shelter for the excess labor force who cannot find alternative employment. The solution for poverty should be found in the creation of spatial and economic conditions for the increase of productivity in the agricultural sector as well as in the non-agricultural sector.

REFERENCES

IBGE, Annuario Estatistico do Ceara. (Various years). Ministerio de Planejamento e Orcamento. Rio de Janeiro, Brazil.

IBGE, Pesquisa Nacional por Amostra de Domicilios (PNAD). (Various years). Ministerio de Planejamento e Orcamento. Rio de Janeiro, Brazil.

IPLANCE. (1999). Rumo ao Desenvolvimento Rural do Ceara, Governo do Estado do Ceara, Brazil.

IPLANCE. (Various years). Anuario Estatistico do Ceara, Secretaria do Planejamento e Coordenacao (SEPLAN). Fortaleza, Ceara, Brazil.

Jentsch, G. (2000). Can economic growth reduce poverty? New findings on inequality, economic growth and poverty. *Development and Cooperation*, *5*, 4–5.

Valdes, A. (1998). *State economic referendum*. Ceara, Brazil: Agriculture and the Rural Sector.

PART II
POLICY APPROACH

CHAPTER 3

AN ASSESSMENT OF POLICIES

We shall now briefly consider the prevailing policies as conceived by various organs of the state and attempt to assess their potential contribution to the reduction of poverty. The analysis here will relate first to macroeconomic policy and later to specific programs in the fields of diminution of poverty, agriculture development, stimulation of non-farm activities, etc. This situation and the policy concept used to confront it are typical not only to the State of Ceara in Brazil, but also to most developing states or countries. We shall show that although such policies generally do contribute to the economic development, they mostly alleviate symptoms and are not sufficient to solve the basic structural problems.

1. GLOBAL MACROECONOMIC POLICY

The macroeconomic policy that prevails in Ceara has been formulated in the "Sustainable Development Plan for Ceara, Brazil, 1995–1998" (see Governo do Estado do Ceara, 1995), and relates both to macroeconomic variables and to regional aspects. Policy measures cover five main vectors. The first one concerns the conservation of nature, specifically state forestation and reforestation, and mainly the fundamental issues of water management: irrigation, basic sanitation, maximizing supply, etc. The second vector addresses the issue of spatial reordering: measures to decrease excessive concentration including regionalized government action, promotion of interior development, redistribution of transportation, energy and communication infrastructures, geological and economic zoning, and urban development programs. The third vector relates to human resource development, and sets targets of universal basic education and education for all, promotion of health, promotion of mature political practices, participatory processes, and fighting poverty. The fourth vector relates to employment generation and economically sustainable development. Relevant strategies address each economic sector. The agricultural sector is supported through utilizing the potential of irrigable land through the development of agro-industrial activities and through the reorganization of the rural economy. Regarding the industrial sector, ventures in the interior of the state are also promoted. The sector of services is promoted through the stimulation of tourism along the coast and in the interior. The fifth and last vector relates to the development of science, technology, and innovation. This is accomplished through the increase of the existing capacity of high-level education in science and technology. Specific programs include generation, diffusion, and innovation oriented by demand, university–industry–society integration, and promotion of centers of excellence.

The growth and structural change indicators mentioned above clearly reveal the efficiency of the macroeconomic policy. The State of Ceara seems to have entered a new phase of development, represented by high growth rates of GDP and GDP per capita, an increasing level of urbanization, growing manufacturing activity, a rapidly developing tourism sector, and a more stabilized fiscal situation.

However, the impressive results of macroeconomic growth are still far from sufficient. The first concern is that Ceara is still one of the poorest states in the country, with less than half of the national GDP per capita. The very important measures taken by the state government should probably be reassessed in terms of their contribution to the productivity of the various sectors of the economy. Measures taken for the improvement of total factor productivity (TFP) are all in the right directions, but still may not be enough.

The second and extremely important concern is that considerable gaps remain between the rural and urban populations of Ceara, and between the metropolitan region of Fortaleza and the interior. The question that naturally arises is: Wouldn't it be possible to achieve a more rapid growth or at least the same rate of growth by increasing the share of poor regions in the development process?

It can be argued (without entering into any detailed elaboration of the question of the relation between growth and distribution) that a dynamic economic growth may naturally result, at least in the short run, in the growing disparities in income distribution. The rationale of this argument is that economic growth is naturally led by the more advanced sectors of the economy, which are in a better position to compete with other economies. Consequently, gains from economic growth are mostly concentrated in these sectors, leading to growing disparities between rich and poor people, and between rich and poor regions. The interior of the country is characterized by a lower level of educational and professional achievement, and by inferior levels of physical, social, and technological infrastructures. Any gains from economic development of the state should therefore be expected to "trickle down" to the interior only at a later stage. However, a few important arguments against this reasoning should be taken into consideration.

First, the "trickle down" argument has not really been proven to be true. Economic growth can happen in one sector and not be entirely diffused to other sectors or regions, thus establishing structural gaps between populations or regions.

Second, the rural sector of Ceara and the interior as a whole, just like peripheral regions in many developing countries suffer from severe structural problems related to land ownership, insufficient infrastructures, lack of know-how, inappropriate social organization, etc. The diffusion of the results of macroeconomic policy to those regions requires as a precondition the adoption of specific policies for the solution of these structural problems.

The macroeconomic policy did recognize the existence of spatial structural problems, which affect the interior and the rural area. However, the policy measures taken both at the macro level and at the local level apparently did not lead to the achievement of the declared objective of regional restructuring. The spatial distribution of the population is still indicative of a rural underdeveloped dichotomic economy. The share of the metropolitan region of Fortaleza in the total population of the state is still increasing, and no signs of urban concentration or consolidation are present in the interior of the state. The lack of a significant process of urban decentralization and the absence of major urban centers in the interior are probably among the most important factors that have slowed the diffusion of economic development to the interior.

The bottom line of this analysis of the macroeconomic policy is that it is quite efficient in the promotion of growth, but insufficient for the diminution of poverty and regional gaps. In order to reach the objective of diminution of poverty together with the objective of state economic growth, two important policy measures should be reconsidered. First, the policy of spatial organization should be revised with an orientation toward the creation of new urban agglomerations (as will be discussed later). Second, more efforts are required in the fields that influence total factor productivity such as public investments in infrastructures, in human capital, in technological advancement, and in institutional organization.

2. RURAL POLICY

The specific policy which is used in Ceara to fight the problems of poverty and of low levels of development in the interior of the state is, as in many other developing countries, oriented primarily toward the solution of focused problems and focused situations in various places (see Leite, 1986, for an analysis of rural development policies in the Northeast region as a whole and of the lessons learned from those policies). In operational terms, this means taking action in three directions. The first could be termed the alleviation of acute economic and social problems by providing support to the population in need of social services, health, education, etc. The second type of action is oriented toward the support of agricultural economic growth through programs of agriculture reform, allocation of land, agricultural extension, etc. The third type of action is oriented toward the support of non-agricultural economic activities. This is done through support programs for industrial activity, provision of basic infrastructures, etc. It would be difficult to classify all the programs that are currently in action or in preparation into these three categories, since each program or even each specific measure may have a direct or indirect impact in different fields. A short presentation of some major programs is included in the "Second Indicative Plan for the Rural Development of Ceara, 1999–2002," as classified by the Secretaria de Desenvolvimento Rural in the "Rumo ao Desenvolvimento Rural do Ceara, 1999–2002" (see also a short survey in Governo do Estado do Ceara, 2000a).

Four major groups of programs are presented: fighting poverty, modernization of traditional agriculture, new opportunities for non-farm employment, and supportive services for agriculture. The financial resources for each group of programs in 1999 and those planned for the period of 1999–2002 are presented in Table 1.

Table 1. Financial Resources for Rural Development Programs, 1999–2002.

	$R (Millions)		Distribution (%)	
	1999	1999–2002	1999	1999–2002
Fighting poverty	115	380	69	66
Modernization of traditional agriculture	48	171	28	29
New opportunities of non-farm employment	0	4	0	1
Government support services for agriculture	5	26	3	4
Total	168	581	100	100

Source: SDR, Rumo ao Desenvolvimento do Ceara (1999–2002); Governo do Ceara, Fortaleza (1999).

As can be seen in the table, most of the financial resources are allocated to programs that are defined as fighting poverty. This first item in the table includes four main projects: the Sao Jose project, the project of support to family farms (PRONAF), the Agrarian Reform Program (Cedula da Terra), and a program of "harvest insurance."

PROJETO SAO JOSE. This program is supported by the World Bank and aims at improving the living conditions of the rural population that suffers most from the acute problems of poverty by decentralizing decision-making processes to municipal and community levels, by providing financial support to organized rural communities, and by stimulating participatory practices. Since its beginning in 1995 and until 1999, this project had already reached more than 5,000 communities in 176 municipalities and provided support to more than 300,000 families (see Governo do Estado do Ceara, 2000a, p. 29).

PRONAF (Programa Nacional de Fortalecimento da Agricultura Familiar): This is a special program for the support of family farms in order to help them increase their production capacity, their employment, and their income. This support includes financing of rural infrastructures and services to help the development of family agriculture.

REFORMA AGRARIA SOLIDARIA – Cedula da Terra: The objective of this program is to develop a new model of agrarian structure, by which the landless workers can buy land through direct negotiation with the rural land owners, with the support of loans for the acquisition of land and grants for investments.

SEGURO SAFRA: This is a program of harvest insurance that was adopted by the Governor of Ceara with the objective of decreasing the negative impacts of droughts on the rural population. It provides a minimum income for a limited period to the farmers who lost at least half of their harvest as a result of a drought. This program was later adopted by the Federal Government of Brazil for all nine states in the Northeast region.

Within this same group of programs, which are primarily directed toward the diminution of poverty, we can also include the PRORENDA: Programa de Apoio a Agricultura Familiar e Pesca Artesanal. This program is financially supported by the German government and its objective is to help communities of small farmers and fishermen to improve their planning and administration of socio-economic activities, with the goal of achieving a sustainable development. Another program is the "HORA DE PLANTAR" or time for planting. This program supports family farms by providing high productivity seeds and by offering education to the farmers.

The second group of projects deals with the modernization of traditional agriculture and requires about 29% of all resources. The objective of this program is to support the modernization of agriculture in non-irrigated lands in order to stimulate private initiative, and increase efficiency and competitive ability. This program concentrates on selected products and regions. It includes support for research and technology transfer.

The group of "Government Support Services for Agriculture" includes technical assistance and rural extension services, rural settlement, food provision, information provision in relation to climate, management and marketing, and control of agricultural products. In sum, these are programs that help increase production, help in the prevention and treatment of various plant and animal maladies, provide sanitation inspection of products of animal origin, provide marketing and alimentary supply, provide laboratory analysis of new seeds, etc. The "Assentamento" or Settlement program assigns state funds for the acquisition of land through a disappropriation process and the settlement of landless rural families (see Governo do Estado do Ceara, 2000b, for a more detailed review of settlement and resettlement programs).

The last group of projects that are included in the "Second Indicative Plan for the Rural Development of Ceara 1999–2002" is the "New Opportunities of Non-Agricultural Employment in the Rural Area" and has a low share of the financial resources. The idea here is to identify the potential for small industries, agri-businesses, production of inputs to agriculture, and production of consumer goods and services for the local population.

The promotion of rural industrialization is the objective of a program under the responsibility of the Secretariat of Economic Development. This program is expected to achieve the establishment of 100 industrial mini-districts in the interior of Ceara.

The policy of rural development that is still being applied actually meets many of the needs of the rural population. The general approach for the achievement of a higher level of economic development and a reduction of poverty and inequality is positive, in principle. It includes the necessary ingredients for a healthy and balanced rural economic development. The measures that are taken within the various programs as described above are oriented toward the support of agricultural activities, the increase of productivity, solution of land allocation problems, building of physical infrastructures, support to education and professional development, stimulation of non-agricultural activities, etc. While this policy has certainly achieved good results in many fields, a few serious problems still require additional consideration.

First, the fact is that there are still enormous gaps between the rural and the urban sector, between the interior and the metropolitan region. The data from the PNAD for 1999 as discussed above shows considerable gaps between the urban sector and the rural sector, between the metropolitan region of Fortaleza and the interior. The fight against poverty may have achieved some results, but those results are still far from being satisfactory.

Second, the specific results of the policy measures for the stimulation of non-agricultural activities are quite poor. The volume of such activities still does not respond to the needs as shown by high levels of unemployment and under-employment. There are no published data on the distribution of employment by economic sectors in the rural area of Ceara, but World Bank evaluations for the Northeast in 1996 (unpublished) show the share of non-agricultural activities as a main occupation reaches only 21.8% in the rural Northeast compared with 31.7% in the rural Southeast, and much higher figures in the rural sector of other Latin American countries. Of the 21.8% of the rural workers in the Northeast who are employed in non-agricultural activities as a main occupation, only 6.3% are employed in industry (compared with 10.1% in the rural Southeast) – mostly in construction, food processing, ceramics, textiles, and wood products. The others are employed in services, mainly private account services, education, food and beverage sales, street sales, and the government. The data concerning employment distribution in the urban area show a higher level of industrialization in the urban Southeast: 25.9% employed in industry (including construction and utilities) compared with 17.5% in the urban Northeast.

Third, the existing indigenous non-farm enterprises represent mostly a first elementary linkage to agricultural activity. Many of them are small-scale activities in the primary processing of agricultural products; many of them still use very elementary processing technology and produce for limited local or regional markets. Those enterprises have limited prospects for growth and stimulation of employment or income multiplier effects. Income data presented above for Ceara as a whole show an indication of this situation. In Ceara, 82% of the workers who are employed in agriculture receive an income earn up to one minimum salary compared with 34% in the Southeast. The data for manufacturing employment is even more alarming: 36% in Ceara are paid an income of up to one minimum salary compared with 7% in the Southeast.

These results raise a few thoughts and questions about the optimal policy for the development of rural areas and for fighting poverty. Before raising these thoughts, we should bear in mind two important considerations. One is that poverty is a direct consequence of low productivity: decreasing poverty implies measures that increase productivity. The second is that there is a strong interdependence between the various components of rural policy with regard to the development of rural agricultural activities, rural non-farm activities, and local urban activities. A more efficient and productive agriculture provides higher levels of income, and therefore sets a threshold for the type of non-farm activities that can be attracted to the region. On the other hand, low levels of income in agriculture enable the existence of low income non-farm activities, in manufacturing or in services. And vice versa: the failure in the development of non-farm activities with an acceptable salary level discourages labor motivation and leads to the growth of disguised unemployment in the rural sector. Therefore, rural policy makes sense as a whole and measures taken in each segment necessarily have an impact on all rural economic activity.

An initial contemplation should be about the rural demographic policy. An accepted assumption is that solutions to rural problems should be provided while keeping the rural population on the land. This is clearly a good policy for preventing the well-known negative implication of the rural-urban migration. Actually, one of the major problems analyzed above, is the problem of the too-rapid growth of the metropolitan region of Fortaleza in relation to the interior. On the other hand, there is no doubt that the constraint of rural exodus may be counter-productive in terms of the fight against poverty. It is clear that economic development is followed by a decrease of agriculture in the total product and in employment. A policy of encouraging the rural population to stay in the rural area can actually lead to negative pressure on agricultural productivity: higher labor intensity and lower technology, higher disguised unemployment, lower productivity, and higher poverty levels. This can be prevented only if the excess rural labor force is employed in non-farm activities. However, the development of such activities is possible to a certain extent within the rural area itself, but requires urban support at later stages. The answer to this dilemma is to relieve the constraint of the objective of keeping the rural population on the land, and at the same time to keep the objective of preventing migration to the metropolitan region and to adopt a policy of diversion of rural-urban migration to urban centers in the interior. This leads us again to the issue of spatial demographic distribution, this time from the rural angle: promoting a policy of development of major urban centers in the interior that would absorb most of the excess labor force from agriculture.

A second thought about the prevailing rural policy is the possible relationship between the policy of land distribution and agricultural productivity. The policy of land reform and redistribution is certainly a good measure for a more equitable distribution of income and for the diminution of poverty levels. However, in some instances there may be a conflict between the redistribution effect and the productivity effect. First, the cost efficiency of a program such as the Reforma Agraria Solidaria is a crucial consideration. In a State Economic Memorandum of the World Bank, Valdes (1998) claims that the need to provide ownership of land, technical assistance, and credit through a highly subsidized program would represent an extraordinarily costly demand on the governmental budget. Second, in the deliberations of a Seminar on the "Agrarian Reform and Sustainable Development" (see Ministerio do Desenvolvimento Agrario, 2000), it is claimed that research findings show that the families who benefited from the agrarian reform did improve their quality of life, but not by much. Many problems of unsustainability and of poverty still persist, due to factors such as the location of lands, the distance to markets, difficult access to infrastructures, etc. In that same seminar, in their analysis of the program of "Cedula da Terra," Buainain and de Silveira (2000) conclude that the existence of a minimal critical mass of family farmers is a fundamental condition for the development of support services. In sum, the land reform program is certainly a good policy (a positive evaluation for the case of Ceara is made in the same seminar by Brandao, 2000), but it should be constrained by considerations of economic efficiency.

A second extremely important economic consideration is the return to the scale of agricultural activity: a too-heavy fragmentation of land may lead to lower productivity levels. Besides the redistribution of land, we should also consider the need to achieve an efficient agriculture, based on a larger scale and improved technologies. The growth of a more efficient agriculture, with higher productivity levels, will necessarily stimulate more productive non-agricultural employment in the region. The support of agricultural activity should therefore be considered not only in terms of its distributive effects and its social impact on deprived populations, but also in terms of its contribution to agricultural productivity. Land allocation should be carefully analyzed, considering the effect of the size of the land on productivity. Such measures should be tested in terms of a possible trade-off between their long-term and short-term effects. Land reform has a positive effect on equality and diminution of poverty in the short-term; large-scale high technology commercial agriculture has long-term effects on rural development, but short-term negative effects on redistribution. An optimal policy should find the appropriate balance between the two.

A third thought is about a policy for the encouragement of rural non-farm employment. The prevailing policy measures provide support for initiatives to develop rural enterprises in relevant fields of infrastructure, training, management, etc. We may characterize these as "responsive" measures to the needs expressed by the local population. This is a correct policy for the assistance of the rural population in its efforts to develop additional activities, and it stimulates bottom-up initiatives and participatory practices. However, such a "responsive" approach may not be sufficient and a more "normative" approach should be considered. The important notion that should be kept in mind in this case is that the development of industrial activities in a region are to a large extent dependent upon external factors that are mostly determined by government policy. For example, a high local demand for industrial investment may result from the construction of a new road or a new industrial park in the region. The "normative" approach should be directed by an external identification by government of optimal places for the stimulation of industrial activities, and by an evaluation of specific and necessary interventions, such as the construction of facilities, the provision of educational facilities, etc. (see Bar-El, 1999, for a general planning model for the evaluation of the required allocation of public expenditures at given policy targets). Such a normative approach is to some extent, behind the policy measures that led, for example, to the establishment of industrial mini-districts. In addition to responding to the needs expressed by specific investors, this normative approach should be guided by the more macroregional long-term interests of industrial development. For example, one consideration is the extent to which we should base rural non-farm employment on small-scale local activities or attract external investments in larger scale activities. In this case, a policy of establishing larger infrastructures should be adopted. A second consideration is the question of whether a constraint should be imposed on investors concerning technological levels. A small low-technology labor-intensive processing plant may answer the needs of the investor, but not the developmental needs of the region as a whole.

The bottom line of this analysis is that the provision of non-farm employment in rural areas is supposed to be an answer to the problems of poverty, but it should mainly be conceived in a much broader context of structural economic change. In addition to the focused treatment of poverty problems in the rural area, a structural approach is needed in terms of normative establishment of human and physical infrastructures, combining the considerations of productivity with those of equal distribution, and combining support for local small-scale non-farm activities with the attraction of external investments in bigger scale industry.

REFERENCES

Bar-El, R. (1999). An iterative approach to regional development planning. In: G. Benhayoun, N. Gaussier, & B. Planque (Eds), *L' Ancrage Territorial du Developpement Durable* (pp. 229–250). L'Harmattan, Paris.

Brandao, W. (2000). A Reforma Agraria Solidaria no Ceara, in Ministerio do Desenvolvimento Agrario: Reforma Agraria e Desenvolvimento Sustentavel, Brazilia.

Buainain, A. M., & de Silveira, J. M. (2000). O Programa Cedula da Terra no Contexto das Novas Politicas de Reforma Agraria, Desenvolvimento e Participacao: uma Discussao das Transformacoes Necessarias e Possiveis. In: Ministerio do Desenvolvimento Agrario: Reforma Agraria e Desenvolvimento Sustentavel, Brazilia.

Governo do Estado do Ceara. (1995). Sustainable development plan of Ceara, Brazil, 1995–1998, Fortaleza, Brazil.

Governo do Estado do Ceara. (1999). Rumo ao Desenvolvimento Rural do Ceara, 1999–2002, Secretaria de Desenvolvimento Rural (SDR), Fortaleza, Ceara, Brazil.

Governo do Estado do Ceara. (2000a). Reforma Agraria no Ceara, Secretaria de Desenvolvimento Rural (SDR), Instituto do Desenvolvimento Agrario do Ceara (IDACE) and Instituto Nacional de Colonizacao e Reforma Agraria (INCRA), Ceara, Brazil.

Governo do Estado do Ceara. (2000b). O Crecimento Rural do Ceara em 1999, Secretaria de Desenvolvimento Rural (SDR), Fortaleza, Ceara, Brazil.

Leite, P. S. (1986). *Forces that will shape future rural development: Northeast Brazil's case*. Fortaleza: Federal University of Ceara.

Ministerio do Desenvolvimento Agrario. (2000). Reforma Agraria e Desenvolvimento Sustentavel, Brazilia.

Valdes, A. (1998). *State economic referendum*. Ceara, Brazil: Agriculture and the Rural Sector.

CHAPTER 4

POTENTIAL AND SCENARIOS

At this stage, we shall evaluate the potential options for rural economic development in Ceara, which can lead to higher levels of non-farm employment, productivity, and a reduction in poverty. The following evaluations will be based first on a global vision of the future of the economic development of Ceara in general, and then of its rural sector in particular, based on historical trends of production, employment and productivity in the main sectors, and alternative policy measures (see Bar-El & Schwartz, 2003). Next, the potential for specific types of non-farm employment will be evaluated.

1. TRENDS OF GROWTH

The trends of growth in total product in Ceara and in each economic sector are shown in Table 1. For the sake of simplicity, we call "agriculture" all crop and cattle or fishing activities; "industry" includes manufacturing, construction, and utilities; and "services" includes all kinds of services, including private and public, economic services, and social services.

A trend line is estimated for each time series using exponential coefficients (the coefficients show the estimated annual rate of growth), where the independent variable x for each year has the value 1 in 1985 and 15 in 1999. First, the product, or value added series are presented. TV stands for total output, IV for industrial output, SV for services output and AV for agricultural output. The estimated equations and their R squares are:

$$\mathrm{TV} = 100\ \mathrm{e}^{0.0337x} \quad R^2 = 0.98$$

$$\mathrm{IV} = 103\ \mathrm{e}^{0.0422x} \quad R^2 = 0.95$$

$$\mathrm{SV} = 99\ \mathrm{e}^{0.0297x} \quad R^2 = 0.99$$

$$\mathrm{AV} = 97\ \mathrm{e}^{0.0108x} \quad R^2 = 0.07$$

From the data and the estimated equations, we can see a consistent total economic growth (very high R square), with an average annual rate of about

Table 1. Indices of Growth by Economic Sector in Ceara: Product, Employment, Productivity (Product per Worker), 1985–1999.

Year	1985	1986	1987	1988	1989	1990	1991	1992	1993	1994	1995	1996	1997	1998	1999
(a) Product															
Total	100	106	110	119	119	121	131	133	134	143	145	150	156	158	162
Agriculture	100	92	88	114	103	99	127	107	76	131	129	134	105	80	125
Industry	100	111	119	127	128	131	141	154	164	158	159	164	180	191	185
Services	100	106	110	114	116	119	123	125	128	133	138	144	150	151	153
(b) Employment															
Total	100	102	103	102	101	100	106	106	111	118	120	115	123	125	132
Agriculture	100	93	83	90	91	89	98	92	97	114	117	103	94	92	109
Industry	100	108	131	96	105	94	94	95	117	107	101	103	119	139	120
Services	100	111	117	121	113	118	123	128	127	127	131	135	163	162	167
(c) Productivity (product per worker)															
Total	100	104	107	117	118	120	123	126	121	121	121	131	127	127	124
Agriculture	100	99	106	126	113	111	130	116	78	115	111	131	111	87	115
Industry	100	103	91	132	121	139	150	162	140	148	157	159	152	137	155
Services	100	96	94	94	103	100	100	97	101	105	105	106	92	93	91

Sources: Calculated on the basis of the Annuario Estatistico do Ceara for years 1985–1997, and preliminary evaluations of IPLANCE for years 1998 and 1999.
1985 = 100.

3.37% (see the coefficient of 0.0337 for TV). This growth of value added is mainly led by industrial growth, at an annual rate of 4.22%, followed by services. The interesting, though not surprising, result in the regression estimations is the fact that the growth of agricultural value added is the only one with an extremely low R square, reflecting the existence of extreme fluctuations in agricultural production. This trend, although not statistically significant, is of a slight annual growth of about 1% over the years.

The trend of growth of employment, and the related trend of growth of productivity (as measured by added value per worker), are evaluated next in the trend lines' estimated regressions.

For employment:

$$\mathrm{TE} = 95\mathrm{e}^{0.0191x} \quad R^2 = 0.88$$
$$\mathrm{IE} = 99\mathrm{e}^{0.0103x} \quad R^2 = 0.14$$
$$\mathrm{SE} = 100\mathrm{e}^{0.0308x} \quad R^2 = 0.87$$
$$\mathrm{AE} = 89\mathrm{e}^{0.0103x} \quad R^2 = 0.23$$

For productivity:

$$\mathrm{TP} = 106e^{0.0146x} \quad R^2 = 0.70$$
$$\mathrm{IP} = 104e^{0.0318x} \quad R^2 = 0.60$$
$$\mathrm{SP} = 99e^{-0.0011x} \quad R^2 = 0.01$$
$$\mathrm{AP} = 109e^{0.0004x} \quad R^2 = 0.00$$

There is a clear trend of growth of about 1.9% a year in total employment (TE). The lower rate of growth of employment compared with value added is, of course, attributed to a growth in productivity (TP), at an annual average rate of about 1.5%. However, examining the behavior of the specific sectors, we find a quite slow and irregular growth of industrial employment (IE), resulting from a relatively rapid increase in productivity levels (IP). The most rapid and steady growth of employment along the years is that of the services (and not of industry, which leads to the economic growth). The growth of employment in this sector should not be misleading, since this is a direct result of stagnation in productivity during the entire 15-year period. Therefore, growth of employment in services reflects, to a large extent, the accumulation of hidden unemployment and low levels of productivity. The sector of agriculture shows the same stagnation in productivity, with a slight trend of employment growth, expressing again constantly growing disguised unemployment levels, and growing levels of poverty.

The main conclusion of this analysis of trends is that additional employment for the solution of poverty problems should be concentrated mainly in the industrial sector. The agricultural and the services sectors have been accumulating high levels of hidden unemployment, with increasing gaps of productivity in relation to industry, and consequently the highest levels of poverty. Increasing production in these sectors may be achieved with the same number of employees, and consequently their productivity will be increased.

2. NON-FARM EMPLOYMENT POTENTIAL: LESSONS FROM A CEARA–NORTHEAST–SOUTHEAST COMPARISON

Using the basis of the economic trends as described above, and given the identified need for non-farm employment, we next evaluate the potential of growth in the rural sector of Ceara. As a point of reference, we shall use data of the distribution of employment between the various sectors in the rural and the urban areas in Ceara, as compared with the Northeast region (NE) and the Southeast region (SE), as presented in Table 2. The source of all data in this table is the PNAD (see above). Data for the Northeast and the Southeast have been computed by Ferreira and Lanjouw (2001) for the year 1996. Data for Ceara was computed by special request to IPLANCE, the statistical unit of the government of Ceara, for the year 1999. Because of technical reasons, the original calculations were effectuated on 1998 PNAD data, and an adaptation was made for the 1999 data of employment by sectors.

The data show a sharp difference between the distribution of employment by main sector of activity in the rural area of Ceara and the Northeast and Southeast regions. Rural employment in the Southeast is based to a large extent (31%) on non-agricultural activities, industry (10%), and services (21%). The share of non-agricultural activities in Ceara is much lower (20%). From a different angle, this means that in Ceara there are 0.26 workers in non-agricultural activities for each worker in agriculture in the rural area (0.28 in the Northeast), while in the Southeast the ratio is 0.45. The non-farm/farm employment ratio in Ceara may be both downward and upward biased. The upward bias (meaning the actual gap between the regions is even greater) is explained by the fact shown above of the existence of large figures of disguised unemployment in the services sector. The downward bias is explained by the existence of disguised unemployment in

Table 2. Distribution of Employed Workers in the Rural and Urban Areas by Main Sector of Employment and by Main Region (%).

	CE (1999)			NE (1996)			SE (1996)		
	Rural (%)	Urban (%)	Total (%)	Rural (%)	Urban (%)	Total (%)	Rural (%)	Urban (%)	Total (%)
Agriculture	79	14	40	78	14	40	69	6	14
Industry	7	19	14	7	18	13	11	26	24
Services	13	68	46	15	68	46	21	68	62
Total	100	100	100	100	100	100	100	100	100

Figures may not total 100% due to rounding.

Sources: (1) For the Northeast and the Southeast in 1996: Ferreira and Lanjouw (2001). (2) For Ceara in 1999: elaboration of primary data of the PNAD for 1998 for each economic branch for the rural and urban areas, and adaptation to data of PNAD 1999, in which the state recovered from a severe drought in 1998.

agriculture. The conclusion is that a healthy rural development in Ceara requires an increase of non-farm activities, together with an increase in productivity in all economic sectors, but mainly the sectors of agriculture and of services that have high rates of disguised unemployment.

Another important perspective is the relationship between economic sectors of activity and spatial rural–urban distribution. A few indicative comparative figures are presented in Table 3.

A higher level of relative specialization in agriculture in Ceara and in the Northeast than in the Southeast can be seen in the table: 14% of the total employed in the urban area work in agriculture as a main occupation, compared with 6% in the Southeast, showing an increasing share of workers who continue working in agriculture while migrating to a city. However, these data do not necessarily indicate a high level of rural–urban economic integration in Ceara. If we consider all agricultural employment and its distribution between rural and city dwellers, we can see in the table that in Ceara and in the Northeast, 20% of all agricultural workers live in the city, while in the Southeast this share reaches 37%. This apparent paradox is explained by the fact that the Southeast is much more urbanized (87% of all the working population) than the Northeast (57%) and Ceara (60%). We conclude, in terms of potential for rural employment development, the following:

1. Agricultural development does not necessarily mean keeping most of the population in the rural areas; it can be achieved alongside a higher rural–urban integration, where a considerable share of the agricultural workers lives in the city.
2. Such a rural–urban integration does not mean a higher relative specialization of the city in agricultural activity; urbanization may imply a rural–urban migration of agricultural workers who continue their employment in agriculture (or it may imply more agricultural initiatives

Table 3. Indicators of Urban and Agricultural Employment by Region, 1999.

	CE (%)	NE (%)	SE (%)
Employed in agriculture in urban area:			
Out of total employed in urban area	14	14	6
Out of total employed in agriculture	20	20	37
Urban share of total employment	60	57	87

Source: Elaboration of PNAD data for 1999.

among the city dwellers), but it mainly implies higher growth-rates of non-agricultural activities.

3. QUANTITATIVE EVALUATION OF NON-FARM EMPLOYMENT POTENTIAL: THE SCENARIO OF "BUSINESS AS USUAL"

The potential of growth of non-farm employment is dependent on a few policy parameters. The main parameters are presented in Table 4, and for each one the prevailing value is shown, as well as an "optimal" value that can be considered by policy makers.

The prevailing trend of agricultural production growth was evaluated above an annual average increase of 1.1%. This rate will also be used for the "business as usual" scenario. The 5% growth-rate is the maximum rate which was mentioned in the indicative plan for agricultural development between 1999 and 2002 (3–5%).

Agricultural productivity growth was evaluated at 0.04% a year, and this is one of the main causes of poverty in the rural area. The optimal rate was set at a productivity growth of 3.2% a year, which is equal to the productivity growth achieved by the industrial sector in Ceara over the last 15 years, as evaluated above. This may be achieved through a combination of growth in capital intensity, agricultural extension, and agricultural structural changes.

Industrial productivity growth, standing at 3.2% over the last several years, is expected to be able to grow to a level of 4%, based on the fact that

Table 4. Limit Values of Parameters for Main Policy Objectives.

Policy Parameters	Business as Usual	Optimal
Agricultural production annual growth	1.1%	5.0%
Annual productivity growth in		
Agriculture	0.04%	3.2%
Industry	3.2%	4.0%
Services	−0.1%	3.2%
Urban share in agricultural employment	20%	38%
Non-farm/farm workers ratio in		
Industry	0.09	0.14
Services	0.17	0.30
Total	0.26	0.45
Urbanization index (employment)	60%	87%

productivity in Ceara is still much less than in other regions in Brazil, as demonstrated above by the income data.

The situation in the sector of services is much more serious. The "business as usual" rate of growth of productivity has stood at about zero for many years. Here again, we assume that productivity growth in this sector can reach the long-term rate of industry, about 3.2%, at least through the diminution of hidden unemployment in this sector.

The share of the urban sector in agriculture is supposed to be able to have long-term growth from the prevailing 20%, toward the share in the Southeast region, which was estimated at 38%. In parallel, the urbanization level, as measured here by the share of workers in the urban area, is expected to grow as it did during the last several years, from 60% toward the maximum of 87% in the Southeast.

The most important parameters relate to non-farm employment. Our evaluations found that 0.26 workers in Ceara are employed in non-farm jobs as their main occupation for every worker in agriculture: 0.70 in industry and 0.19 in services. The rate in the Southeast is 73% greater, as evaluated on the basis of the PNAD data by the Ferreira and Lanjouw (2001) study: 0.45 workers for each worker in agriculture. This figure will serve as a criterion in our calculations.

The results of a few alternatives for rural development for a period of 5 years, based on the "business as usual" scenario are shown in Table 5.

The first column of numbers presents the situation in the year 1999, in relation to main relevant variables. The actual number of workers in agriculture (1,277,000 workers) was not used, since this number suffers from heavy annual fluctuations. Instead, the trend estimated number (see above) is used (1,220,000) as a basis for the estimates of year 2004. The share of urban workers in agriculture (250,000) is evaluated on the basis of latest PNAD data. On the same basis, the number of rural workers in industry (91,000) and in services (161,000) was evaluated, leading to the total number of rural workers in Ceara (1,222,000 workers). This is slightly lower than the figure of total workers, due to differences caused by calibration of time series to the evaluated trends.

The first option, "business as usual" with no intervention, displays the expected changes in the values of all the variables, on the basis of the above estimated coefficients. The trend of a slight annual increase of 1.1% in agricultural production is expected to lead to additional employment for about 65,000 workers in 2004 (assuming a continuation of the stagnating productivity), of which 51,000 are in the rural area. "Business as usual" would also lead to about 11,000 additional jobs in non-farm activities in the

Table 5. "Business as Usual" Scenario and Alternative Equilibria in a 5-Year Period.

Policy Parameters	"Business as Usual" Equilibrated by:								
		No intervention		Rural–urban migration		Non-farm employment		Combined	
Agricultural production annual growth		1.1%		1.1%		1.1%		1.1%	
Annual productivity growth in:									
Agriculture		0.0%		0.0%		0.0%		0.0%	
Industry		3.2%		3.2%		3.2%		3.2%	
Services		−0.1%		−0.1%		−0.1%		−0.1%	
Urban share in agricultural employment		20.5%		20.5%		20.5%		20.5%	
Non-farm/farm workers ratio in:									
Industry		0.09		0.09		0.11		0.10	
Services		0.17		0.17		0.21		0.18	
Total		0.26		0.26		0.32		0.28	
Urbanization index (employment)		60.0%		61.8%		60.0%		61.2%	
Evaluated results	1999	2004	dif.	2004	dif.	2004	dif.	2004	dif.
Agricultural employment index	104	109	6	109	6	109	6	109	6
Agricultural workers (thousands)	1,220	1,285	65	1,285	65	1,285	65	1,285	65
Of which: urban	250	263	13	263	13	263	13	263	13
Rural employment in:									
Agriculture	970	1,021	51	1,021	51	1,021	51	1,021	51
Industry	91	93	2	93	2	109	17	99	8
Services	161	170	9	170	9	214	53	184	23
Rural employment balance:									
Demand (growth of workers)	1,233	1,355	122	1,295	62	1,355	122	1,315	82
Supply (farm and non-farm)	1,222	1,284	62	1,284	62	1,345	122	1,304	82
Expected excess labor force			60		0		0		0

rural area: 2,000 in industry (assuming continuation of the productivity trend in this sector), and 9,000 in services. This results in an increase of 62,000 jobs in the rural area, while the demand for employment is expected to increase at the same time by 122,000 persons (assuming continuation of the same trends). The final results of the "business as usual" scenario are therefore:

1. 60,000 additional persons in the rural area who have no jobs, and join open or hidden unemployment.
2. 1,284,000 employed in the rural area, about 1 million of whom are in agriculture as a main occupation, with more or less the same levels of low productivity as before.

This means there is no change in the poverty levels for the existing population, and an addition of thousands of persons with no employment, leading to a significant worsening of the average situation in the following years.

The first option, equilibrium through rural–urban migration, assumes that the excess labor force of 60,000 workers will migrate to the city, leading to an increase of the urbanization level (measured in terms of workers) to 61.8%. This actually reflects the actual trend of urbanization in the past few decades.

The second option for equilibrium is the supply of non-farm employment, preventing rural–urban migration. This option requires a significant growth of non-farm activities: the additional jobs would have to increase by 17,000 in the industrial sector (compared with only 2,000 without intervention), and by 53,000 in the services sector (instead of 9,000). The ratio of non-farm to farm employment increases from 0.26 to 0.32, both still much lower than the ratio in Southeast.

The final option combines both the stimulation of non-farm employment and the existence of some rural–urban migration.

We should remember that all these options are based on a "business as usual" scenario, meaning that they relate only to the additional needs that may arise in the next few years, but without taking any significant measures to change productivity. All measures in this section were only meant to solve the additional problems expected in the coming years, without improving the existing situation.

4. QUANTITATIVE EVALUATION OF NON-FARM EMPLOYMENT POTENTIAL: THE SCENARIO OF "PRODUCTIVITY GROWTH"

Solving the problem of poverty means not only solving the problem of unemployment, but also, and most important, that of low productivity. Full employment in low productivity jobs would supply low levels of income and limit the ability to solve the poverty problem. The existing gaps in income levels, as calculated and analyzed above, require drastic improvements in productivity levels.

We will not enter here into all the required measures for improving productivity (this will be the subject of the next section). Instead, at this time we evaluate the maximum possible changes of productivity, and calculate the implications on the need for the creation of non-farm employment, as presented in Table 6.

In this scenario, we use the "optimal" productivity levels as assumed above: a growth of 3.2% in the productivity of agriculture and of services (instead of a practically zero growth in productivity in the last 15 years), and 4.0% in industry (instead of 3.2%). Productivity growth is expected to lead to higher levels of income, but it should be remembered that at given levels of demand for the product, it means a reduction of demand for workers. The first option (without equilibrium) presented in Table 6 shows the results of a potential improvement in productivity in the three sectors, but still

Table 6. "Productivity Growth" Scenario and Alternative Equilibriums in 2004.

Policy Parameters	Productivity Growth, Equilibrated by:				
	Without equilibrium	Urbanization	Non-farm employment	Agricultural growth	Combined
Agricultural production annual growth	1.1%	1.1%	1.1%	5.2%	3.0%
Annual productivity growth in:					
Agriculture	3.2%	3.2%	3.2%	3.2%	3.2%
Industry	4.0%	4.0%	4.0%	4.0%	4.0%
Services	3.2%	3.2%	3.2%	3.2%	3.2%
Urban share in agricultural employment	20.5%	20.5%	20.5%	20.5%	22.0%
Non-farm/farm workers ratio in:					
Industry	0.09	0.09	0.19	0.09	0.10
Services	0.17	0.17	0.35	0.17	0.20
Total	0.26	0.26	0.54	0.26	0.30
Urbanization index (employment)	60.0%	67.2%	60.0%	60.0%	63.6%

Evaluated results	1999	2004	dif.	2004	dif.	2004	dif.	2004	dif.	2004	dif.
Agricultural employment index	104	94	−10	94	−10	94	−10	114	10	103	−1
Agricultural workers (thousands)	1,220	1,101	−119	1,101	−119	1,101	−119	1,343	123	1,209	−11
Of which: urban	250	226	−24	226	−24	226	−24	275	25	266	16
Rural employment in:											
Agriculture	970	875	−95	875	−95	875	−95	1,067	98	943	−27
Industry	91	82	−10	82	−10	165	73	100	8	90	−1
Services	161	145	−16	145	−16	305	144	177	16	189	28
Rural employment balance:											
Demand (growth of workers)	1,233	1,355	122	1,113	−120	1,355	122	1,355	122	1,233	0
Supply (farm and non-farm)	1,222	1,102	−120	1,102	−120	1,345	122	1,345	122	1,222	0
Expected excess labor force			242		0		0		0		0

without any increase in product demand. In this case, the excess of labor reaches 242,000 persons in the year 2004. This is due to the fact that the improved productivity leads primarily to a sharp decrease in workers in agriculture: a decrease of 119,000 workers in 5 years (95,000 agricultural workers in the rural area), instead of an increase of 65,000 in the case of an unchanged trend in productivity. This means that the number of workers in agriculture would decrease by about 10% in relation to its level in 1999, reflecting a diminution of hidden unemployment and an improvement in productivity. The number of workers in non-farm activities is also expected to decrease in this scenario by 10,000 in industry and 16,000 in services, due to the increased productivity in conditions of a regular growth in demand, following past trends.

In free market conditions, and assuming that nothing else happens besides the increase in productivity, this would lead to an increase of unemployment by 242,000 persons, out of the expected labor force of 1,355,000 persons, or about 20% unemployment. However, the assumption that "nothing else happens" is not reasonable. If no other measure is taken besides improving productivity, some of the new excess workers will stay on their jobs, mainly in the agricultural sector, and actually join the informal category of "hidden unemployment." This would mean a statistical decline of the productivity measures, as defined by product per worker. We shall consider now a few strategies for the achievement of an economically healthy balance in the rural area, as shown in the table above.

5. STRATEGIES

The first alternative solution to solving the problem of this excess labor force as presented in Table 6 is urbanization. In this case, equilibrium would be achieved by the migration of 242,000 workers from the rural area to the urban area. This would lead to an increase of the urbanization index from 60 to 67.2%, within a period of 5 years. In absolute terms, we could divide this number into two equal parts: about 120,000 persons who joined the labor force as a consequence of the natural growth, and the same number of persons who are dismissed from their jobs as a result of the increased productivity.

Is this solution reasonable? The historical trend of rural–urban migration as shown in an earlier section leads to more or less absolute stability in rural population. This means that the same continuing pattern would lead to the growth of the urbanization index from 60% to about 63.6% in 2004, which would be more or less coherent with the regular historical trend of growth of urbanization. The result obtained here is that the solution of rural–urban migration would double the flow of migrants, and lead to a decrease in the absolute rural population by about 10%: from a population of 1.222 million workers in 1999 to 1.102 million in 2004.

The second alternative solution is one of stimulation of non-farm employment in order to increase labor demand, substituting for the decreasing demand resulting from higher productivity, and preventing workers from migrating to the urban area. In order to achieve this goal, the number of non-farm workers should increase by about 80% within 5 years: from 91 to 165,000 in industry, and almost double from 161 to 305,000 in services. Since at the same time the number of agricultural workers is expected to decrease as a result of higher productivity, this means a ratio of 0.54 workers in non-farm employment for each worker in agriculture, or double the prevailing rate. This ratio is much greater than the ratio in the Southeast region (0.45), and therefore is apparently not realistic.

The third alternative for achieving equilibrium while increasing productivity is by increasing agricultural production. The rate of growth of demand for agricultural production which was evaluated as necessary in order to prevent migration (assuming the ratio of non-farm to farm employment is kept constant) is 5.2% a year. This is a slightly higher rate of growth than the rate that was set as a target in the indicative agricultural plan of the SDR for the years 1999 to 2002. At this rate, agricultural production would grow by about 29% in 5 years. Given the productivity growth targets, this would be achieved by a growth of about 10% in agricultural employment, which would be followed by an equal growth of non-farm employment. Growth in agricultural productivity is certainly expected to lead to a greater competitive ability of the agricultural products of Ceara, and to more exports of these products to other states in or outside Brazil (an annual growth of 5.2% in agricultural production is way beyond the absorption capacity of the local market). If actual agricultural production is achieved mainly by increased productivity in the sector, the resulting competitive growth may also lead to agricultural import substitution (from other states). The local demand for many agricultural products, both for direct consumption and for inputs to industrial processing, now depends on imports from other regions. This is true mainly for cotton, corn, rice, and milk. However, this is certainly an enormous challenge, one which requires fierce competition with present suppliers of imports and a rapid penetration into foreign markets, and generally requires long-term preparations.

The last "combined" alternative is probably the most feasible one, since it combines policies at apparently reasonable rates. Here are the main components of this policy package:

1. Set as a policy target an increase of agricultural production at the level of 3% a year, which is the lower boundary of the indicative plan of the SDR. Compared with the trend of 1.1% annual growth in agricultural production, the supply of agricultural jobs will increase by 108,000, from 1.101 million to 1.209 million. Still, this means that the increasing agricultural production would be a result of the investments in increasing agricultural productivity, with no increase (and even a slight decrease) in agricultural employment compared with the present situation.
2. Accept a continuation of the rural–urban migration trend, leading to absolute stability in rural population, and to an increase of the urbanization index from 60 to 63.6%. This would be followed by a slight increase in the share of urban workers in agricultural employment.
3. The ratio of non-farm to farm employment that is required to achieve full equilibrium would increase by about 15%, from 0.26 today to 0.30 in 5 years. This is far from the 0.45 ratio in the Southeast, but still quite feasible given the expected improvement in productivity. The number of additional jobs in non-farm activities would reach about 27,000 in 5 years, which is similar to the reduction of the number of workers expected in agriculture in the rural area.

6. CONCLUSION: A COMBINED STRATEGY

Solving the problem of rural poverty in Ceara is not beyond reach, but it can hardly be achieved by any separate instrument. The potential for rural development is directly linked with the combined potential of a number of components: increasing productivity, increasing demand for agricultural production, increasing non-farm employment, and increasing urbanization in the interior. The potential effect of each of these components is not sufficient for the solution of the rural poverty problem, while the use of all of them in a coherent way provides the necessary synergy for the achievement of a healthy economic growth.

Such a synergy can be generated only if the implementation of all the components is coordinated in an appropriate way. In order to achieve this, the full commitment of the government and coordination among its various branches are important pre-conditions. Furthermore, since the nature of such a synergy has not yet been fully identified in detail, a continual follow-up and analysis of the interaction effects will be necessary.

1. *Increasing rural productivity and agricultural production*: There is a potential for increased productivity in all economic sectors, and mainly in agriculture and services, where productivity levels are extremely low. Our evaluations show a potential for increased productivity of 3 to 4% a year, leading to a parallel increase in income. Increased productivity may be increased by the policy measures of education, training, and infrastructures as will be discussed later, but it also can result from measures that offer attractive alternatives to workers in sectors with high hidden unemployment levels. Our analysis shows that increasing productivity leads to an excess of about 242,000 workers. However, increasing productivity may be useless without complementary measures for absorbing the excess labor force. Higher agricultural productivity does not necessarily mean higher total agricultural production. The quantity of agricultural product depends on supply–demand factors. The same level of agricultural demand means lower employment levels in agriculture as a result of higher productivity. The planned growth of 3% a year in agricultural production is much beyond the projected local demand increase and can be implemented only by increasing agricultural exports. The increased productivity in agriculture can certainly contribute to the competitiveness of this sector in national and international markets. Such growth in agricultural production provides about 108,000 jobs to persons who lost their jobs because of increased productivity. Still, agriculture would demand 11,000 fewer workers than in the present;
2. *Non-farm employment*: The stimulation of non-farm employment can contribute to the supply of additional jobs, but not as a separate measure. The required number of non-farm jobs for the absorption of the excess labor force is not reasonable, as it would lead to a too high non-farm to farm employment ratio. The growth potential of non-farm employment is calculated at about 27,000 new workers in 5 years, increasing the prevailing non-farm to farm employment ratio by about 15%. This number of additional workers is similar to the number of workers that would be released from agriculture; and
3. *Urbanization*: Keeping the entire rural population in the rural area is an unrealistic objective. The potential of all the above components leads to about 122,000 new jobs, which is half the excess labor force. A balanced

solution requires the rural–urban migration of the same number of workers. The meaning of such migration is that more or less all growth in rural population would migrate, and therefore that the absolute size of the rural population would remain the same. This is actually what has happened in the last few decades, and therefore a process of organized urbanization seems quite feasible. Finally, as will be discussed at a later stage, we should indicate that this component also acts in synergy with the others: higher levels of urbanization are expected to support the stimulation of non-farm employment and even the growth of agriculture in the rural area.

While the need for such a combined strategy seems to be clear, the actual translation of such a strategy into detailed planning terms should be further investigated. In terms of the theoretical aspects, the existence of a synergy between the three main components still has to be tested and quantified. The existence of an interaction between the components may require delicate coordination between the timing of their implementation.

Although this strategy is based on theoretical considerations, it has been derived from thc spccific cmpirical data of the State of Ceara. This means that it is appropriate mainly for the conditions of this specific case – basically, the existence of a considerable agricultural rural sector, the existence of a primate city, the existence of a basis for urban growth out of the metropolis, and the dedication of the government toward a solution of the poverty and inequality question. Although this approach may be generalized to some extent, its applicability should be tested for the specific conditions in each case (Friedmann, 2005), and adaptations should consequently be considered.

REFERENCES

Bar-El, R., & Schwartz, D. (2003). Economic growth, inequality and spatial demographic distribution: A Brazilian case. *Revue Région et Développement*, *18*, 147–170.

Ferreira, F. H. G., & Lanjouw, P. (2001). Rural non-farm activities and poverty in the Brazilian Northeast. *World Development*, *29*(3), 509–528.

Friedmann, J. (2005). Globalization and the emerging culture of planning. *Progress in Planning*, *64*(3), 177–234.

CHAPTER 5

POLICY APPROACH AND IMPLEMENTATION

1. THE APPROACH: SOLVING MARKET FAILURES IN THE INTERIOR, WITH MEASURES AT THE NATIONAL, REGIONAL, AND LOCAL LEVEL

The policy approach adopted by the State of Ceara relies basically on the fundamental evaluation revealed above that a major factor influencing poverty and inequality is the existence of a structural market failure in the process of economic development. This failure leads to a situation where structural changes in the economy, such as the diminution of the relative weight of agriculture, are not followed by appropriate adaptations of the society in terms of transition of the labor force to new types of employment, or in terms of urbanization and spatial restructuring. If this is actually a market failure, this implies that the "natural" free market action does not lead to an optimum in the state economy. The intervention of the State in this case is needed in order to achieve a better economic optimum. This means that the government policy that would lead to a reduction of poverty and of inequality would lead at the same time to a larger and more efficient macroeconomic growth.

We emphasize again that we focus here on the solution of problems of poverty and inequality that result from the economic development process; we do not deal here with problems that can be alleviated only through social assistance measures, such as the poverty of an older population or of a population with serious health constraints.

Let us point to the main failures that were indicated in previous chapters, and explain why, in principle, these are market failures that require the intervention of the State government:

1. The relative size of the population in the main metropolitan region of Fortaleza increases constantly, but this does not necessarily reflect the existence of a healthy economic response to a growth process: there is high unemployment and weak social infrastructures

2. The other urban centers in the interior of the State do not respond to the natural urbanization processes that should result from a transition from agricultural to industrial and service activities; and
3. The rural area does not reveal any healthy free market response to changes in the economic structure: although there is some rural–urban migration, the labor force does not respond to the lack of employment in agriculture by a transition to cities or by the development of non-farm activities. The fact is that the share of agriculture is much less than the share of labor force in the rural area, leaving space for high levels of unemployment, under-employment, and low productivity. This is due to the fact that the natural free market alternative responses that could lead to an optimum do not function:
   (a) Migration to the metropolitan region of Fortaleza is not always feasible: the demand for labor is not high enough there and most of the excess labor force in the rural area do not have the necessary economic potential for migration.
   (b) Migration to a small city in the region is not always feasible because those cities do not have the potential to absorb new populations and new economic activity.
   (c) Development of rural non-farm activities is limited by the lack of access to appropriate infrastructures, services, and human capital.

These bottlenecks are not solved by the action of the free market, because of the prevalence of a typical market failure: the free market development of activities such as non-farm enterprises or industrial firms in small cities is hindered by the existence of positive externalities. Private investments may not be viable in the short term because of the lack of amenities such as infrastructures, services, and human capital, while:

1. The development of such activities may induce externalities by increasing income in the region, increasing demand for labor force, increasing demand for local inputs, improving the quality of labor force, etc.
2. Investments in infrastructures and in human capital may be viable in the long run for the region as a whole, even if they are not viable for the private investor in the short run.

This is a typical situation that requires the intervention of the state in the economy, in order to achieve a better social optimum, in terms of economic benefits to the society as a whole. Such intervention should be oriented toward the solution of market failures. However, the specific package of measures to be taken by the government should be carefully analyzed and adapted to the given conditions in order to achieve maximum effectiveness. Treating the problem of poverty and inequality through economic development requires both a clear macroeconomic policy and a focused local policy. The natural long-term trends, such as the decline of the relative weight of agriculture in economic growth and globalization processes, impose serious challenges. The rural area and the interior as a whole must adapt to the changing economic structures and develop the ability to compete in an increasingly industrializing and modernizing economy. This is a new situation for a population that was generally used to a quite closed economy (and in many cases, a subsistence economy).

The general concept is, therefore, that the solution of poverty and inequality in the rural area through the promotion of non-farm employment cannot be achieved only by focused local efforts. It also requires measures on a much wider scale. Economic development in the rural area, beyond the supply of local needs, requires first the solution of bottlenecks that generally constrain the ability to achieve acceptable levels of productivity: infrastructures, human capital, institutional frameworks, access to finance, access to markets, access to know-how and technology. But, in addition, achieving competitive ability also requires appropriate exogenous conditions such as support of an appropriate urban structure in the interior. Also, the changing economic structures (the decrease of the relative weight of agriculture in the economy) imply the need for demographic changes, in terms of urbanization processes.

We can therefore summarize the approach of the government of Ceara for the achievement of growth together with equality and diminution of poverty as one that is focused on the solution of market failures at the following levels:

1. Spatial restructuring, in terms of reinforcement of the urban structure in the interior of the state. This is expected to facilitate economic development and attract excess labor force to industrial and service activities.
2. Supporting regional collaboration, through the stimulation of appropriate organizations, in order to induce agglomeration economies.
3. Stimulate the increase of productivity at the microeconomic level, through the improvement of access to education and public services, stimulation of entrepreneurship, and support of technological improvement.

The expected consequences of such a policy approach would be:

1. The creation of a higher supply of employment opportunities to the rural population in nearby cities.

2. The deviation of migration, decreasing the number of migrants to the metropolitan region of Fortaleza, and increasing the number of migrants to local cities, leading to more balanced growth of Fortaleza.
3. The decrease of excess labor force in the rural area, leading to greater productivity levels and higher income levels.

The approach for the solution of poverty is therefore one that considers the interior as an economic unit, and not as a burden on the State economy to be handled with transfer payments only. The policy guidelines for the solution of the problem of economic development of the interior are therefore focused on the replacement of a dichotomic approach by an integration of the economy of the interior into the State economy. The policy is then oriented toward the inducement of a dynamic endogenous economic growth in the interior as a whole, in coherence with the economic growth of the State.

Such policy guidelines are illustrated in the following figure (Fig. 1).

The first guideline is urban restructuring in the interior, by stimulating the development of secondary cities and regional towns. Urban development within the interior would enable a stronger relationship between the economy of the interior and that of the metropolitan region.

The second guideline relates to the reinforcement of the local economy of the interior (both at the rural and at the local urban levels), by the adoption of

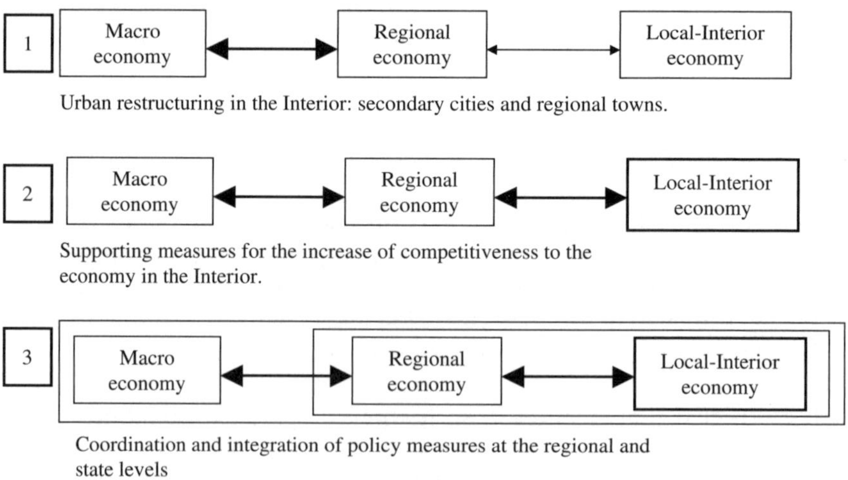

Fig. 1. Policy Guidelines.

measures for the solution of bottlenecks, such as the lack of infrastructures, the low levels of human capital, the access to capital and to markets. Such measures would be facilitated by the support of a more developed urban structure in the interior, as described in the first guideline.

The third guideline relates to the coordination and integration of policy measures at the local and regional (urban) levels with the central state level. The establishment of a regional economic development unit system would assure the consolidation of all the policy measures within the local level, integration between the development of the local and the regional levels, and coherence between the economic development in the interior and the central national economic policy.

The recent history of public policy in the State of Ceara already shows a strong priority to measures improving the human capital, supporting agricultural development, and upgrading infrastructures, together with measures for attracting industrial investments. This has been true in the last couple of decades, and emphasized in the last few years since the beginning of the new millennium. The comprehensive policy including integrated measures of regional restructuring together with regional organization and with the solution of bottlenecks at the local level has been adopted by the Government of Ceara during the first year of the new millennium. Some of the measures that already prevailed were continued or reinforced, new ones were added gradually.

2. ORGANIZATIONAL STRUCTURE

The project of regional development as adopted by the Government of Ceara has a main objective of alleviation of poverty in the interior and the reduction of inequalities between the interior and the metropolitan region.

In the framework of this project, a few programs are already under way at the national, regional, and local levels, as will be described in more detail in the following chapters:

- the establishment of a new Secretariat for local and regional development (SDLR),
- the establishment of Regional Offices and Regional Councils, under the umbrella of the SDLR,
- a program of regional urban restructuring,
- a program of monitoring for small- and medium-sized enterprises in the interior,

- a program for technological promotion in the interior, and
- other programs that are still in an elaboration or pilot phase, such as the advance of entrepreneurship in the agricultural sector, projects of rural industrialization, the establishment of technological and entrepreneurship networks, etc.

An extremely important feature of this project is the high level of commitment of the government in its implementation: since it was first initiated by the Secretary of Rural Development Pedro Sisnando Leite, with the participation of Secretaries Monica Clark and Carlos Matos, the governor of the State at this time, Tasso Jereissati, provided a full endorsement of the project. The newly elected Governor Lucio Alcantara and his government stated their clear commitment to the main objectives of the project and to the approach used until now, and are actively taking all the necessary measures for implementation.

The whole project of regional development is guided by a Conselho Gestor (CG), headed by the Vice-Governor, and including the Secretaries of Local and Regional Development (SDLR), Labor and Entrepreneurship (SETE), Science and Technology (SECETE), Agriculture (SEAGRI), the President of the Institute for Economic Research in Ceara (IPECE), and Prof. Pedro Sisnando Leite, who was the first initiator of this program as Secretary of Rural Development (SDR). The CG is the highest authority and is responsible for the project. The CG takes all decisions on policy measures. The CG meets periodically, receives reports from all programs, and takes decisions about continuation.

The CG is assisted by a Directoria do Projeto (DP), operating within the department of Coordination of Regional Development – CODER – established within the SDLR. The DP includes professionals who are responsible for the actual operation of the project, by coordinating and monitoring the actions of the specific projects. The DP has two roles: one of coordination and monitoring and one of continuous evaluation. The DP reports to the CG once a month for its mensal meetings. The DP has full responsibility for the continuous action and evaluation of the programs, and is expected to immediately report to the CG in case of any problem or bottleneck in the functioning of any specific program.

Each of the programs above is guided by a separate steering committee or a council of secretaries: the Conselho dos Escritorios Regionais (CER), the Conselho dos PDRs (CPDR), the Conselho da Consultoria Empresarial (CCE), the Conselho do Avanco Tecnologico (CAT), etc. The list of secretaries who take part in each of those Councils is decided by the CG. Each of the Councils meets once a month.

Each of the specific programs has a Program Coordinator (Coordenador do Programa, CP) who is in charge of running the program, relating to the relevant Council, and coordinating with the DP.

The following chapters will deal with the specific programs that are being implemented by the State, in coherence with the guidelines mentioned above.

3. IMPLEMENTATION: CRITERIA FOR THE SELECTION OF PROJECTS

The solution of market failures by the government takes the concrete form of budget allocation and implementation of specific actions. The transition from the conceptual approach of solving a market failure to the adoption and implementation of actual concrete measures is not trivial. The concrete actions taken by government are actually specific projects in which it participates. The important question to be answered now is how to select from the various project ideas those that are most cost-effective from the point of view of solving market failures. A critical phase in the implementation of regional development plans is therefore the selection of projects to be supported and the decision about the type of support that should be offered to those projects.

A few conceptual principles have been elaborated, as follows.

1. The basic approach: the selection of projects to be supported by government in one way or another should be guided by the essential contention that those projects make a substantive contribution to the well-being of the society of the region as a whole in the short term or in the longer term (in terms of economic benefits or others), and that this contribution could not be achieved without the support of government. Support to projects that increase benefits to an entrepreneur with no contribution to the society should be avoided. In concrete terms, the basic criteria for the selection of projects to be supported could be:
   (a) The existence of market failures that are linked with the lack of access to resources or services that are normally provided by the government, such as the lack of appropriate infrastructures, insufficient education and professional training services, and limited access to public services such as consultancy or administrative services.

(b) The existence of positive externalities, which are created by the project, therefore generating benefits to the society beyond the benefits of a private firm. In such cases the project may not be economically viable for the individual firm, since only direct benefits are considered, but could be economically or socially viable for the society in the region as a whole. Furthermore, even a project that is economically viable on an individual basis may be supported if such support may generate growth of the project and increase benefits to the society.

(c) The prevalence of an "infant industry" argument: projects which are not economically viable in the short term but need assistance for a limited period of time until they reach maturity and then achieve economic viability.

2. Given the guidelines above, projects that contribute to the reinforcement of local governance and projects that support the creation of a dynamic endogenous process of growth should be prioritized.
3. The consideration of the existence of a "revealed local entrepreneurship" as shown by the existence of activities that are already developed should not necessarily be a major and critical factor in the decision to support a project. New projects should be considered as well, even if no previous experience has been accumulated, if such new projects respond to the basic criteria mentioned above. Giving a strong priority to "revealed local entrepreneurship" could prevent or at least restrict the development of new initiatives that respond to the new conditions in the interior, and lead to a stronger concentration in economic activities that were justified by past conditions that are no more relevant.
4. It is a good policy not to offer support as a global package, but to focus on specific problematic points. However, the existence of a bottleneck or the specific necessity for certain infrastructures or machinery or equipment should not be necessary or sufficient condition for government support. A support for the solution of such bottlenecks should be considered only if the other basic conditions for support are met: in many cases, the mere existence of a bottleneck may be a symptom of the existence of some major inefficiency in the firm, and its solution may actually promote an inappropriate economic activity.
5. The priority sometimes given to the poorest municipalities can be justified only in the context of a "social assistance" approach as implemented by the Sao Jose project. An approach which is more oriented toward long-term economic growth and efficiency in the interior may imply the preference of other municipalities, but with a heavy social cost of lower priority to poor municipalities.

6. "Arranjo Produtivo Local" (APL): the existence of a Local Production Complex (whether it is defined as a cluster of activities or as an economic sector that includes activities of similar kind) may certainly be a good basis for the economic growth of a region. The support to economic activities that are part of such APL may be justified by the multiplier effects that are generated, and by the fact that income leakages and employment leakages to other regions are diminished. However, it should be remembered that imposing the existence of such an APL as a condition for government support may be counter-productive in many cases. The existence of an APL may be an efficient factor for the promotion of positive externalities, and therefore should be considered whenever such externalities are actually present. Still, the existence of an APL may result from historical economic developments and may be less appropriate in view of new economic situations: diminution of the weight of agriculture, higher levels of education, better infrastructures, urban restructuring, technological advance, etc. Therefore, we believe that the priority given to APLs along the document should be relieved to a certain extent. The existence of an APL may be a criterion for the selection of a project if it responds to the basic conditions described above, but it should certainly not prevent or even decrease the chances of support to new economic activities that are not a part of an APL but do respond to the new expected conditions in the region, and to the basic conditions stated above.
7. The support provided by the government to a project can be in the form of grants that are not reimbursable, but this should not necessarily be the rule in all other projects. A special chapter is dedicated later to the issue of types of incentives.
8. Criteria for the elimination of projects: basically, projects that do not fit the basic conditions stated above should be eliminated. In concrete terms, a project should not be considered if:
   (a) The public support does not generate any added value beyond the benefits to the entrepreneur (cases where the project could exist and generate the same benefits without the intervention of the state).
   (b) The project cannot exist in the longer term without public support, and the project generates positive externalities.
9. Channels of public support: the types of support offered should be elaborated as a function of the specific conditions that justify the support. In general terms:
   (a) Solving market failures linked to government activities or other institutional activities: support should be in terms of the solution of

failures such as construction of infrastructures, provision of education facilities, generally (but not always fully) covered by the government.

(b) Existence of positive externalities: the government should participate in the investment and/or in some costs and/or in tax exemptions, partially as a function of the level of externalities that are generated.

(c) Infant industries: partial support in investment or in current costs, but with a time limit of about 3–5 years, decreasing gradually.

PART III
REGIONAL RESTRUCTURING – MACRO-REGIONAL POLICY

CHAPTER 6

SPATIAL POLICY: URBANIZATION AND THE PRINCIPLE OF "CONCENTRATED DISPERSION"

The spatial organization of the population distribution is an integral part of the policy strategy for rural development and the fight against poverty. An appropriate spatial distribution and organization of the population may directly affect the emerging economic structure in the interior, the feasibility of various economic activities, the productivity levels, the access of labor force to employment, the access to markets, etc.

1. POLICY CONCEPT

The policy for spatial organization considers three levels: the first is the distribution between the rural and urban populations, the second is the distribution of the urban population between the metropolitan region and the interior, and the third is the spatial organization of the urban population in the interior.

1.1. Rural–Urban Distribution

Migration of the rural population to metropolitan centers has led to enormous problems both in the main city and in the rural area itself, and has in many cases resulted in a policy of "keeping the rural person on his land." This may be a too extreme solution for the rural–urban migration problem. The continuous decrease of the share of agriculture in the economy, the decreasing rural population needed to provide agricultural production, and the need to increase agricultural productivity by producing the same limited quantities of agricultural products with fewer workers, all explain why it is impossible to keep all the people on their land. Doing so would be counter-productive in terms of the fight against poverty; this would increase disguised unemployment and low productivity. The findings of our combined policy in the productivity growth scenario actually indicate the need for rural migration to cities, in quite significant numbers, and a continuation of the process of urbanization.

1.2. Metropolitan–Interior Urban Distribution

Urbanization without increasing metropolitan concentration implies the development and growth of cities in the interior or the "interiorization of urbanization." The idea would be the building of small cities or townships in proximity to agricultural areas, in order to provide support for agriculture and to develop non-farm employment opportunities (Rondinelli & Ruddle, 1978). The need for a more equilibrated spatial distribution of the population and of economic activity has already been recognized in the "Sustainable Economic Plan of Ceara." Since most of the rural non-farm employment is expected to be in the fields of manufacturing and services, and not necessarily related to agricultural activity, a process of urbanization of the interior can be expected. The comprehensive study of "Rural Industrialization in the Northeast of Brazil" (Banco do Nordeste do Brazil, 1978) revealed two decades ago that non-farm employment is more easily achieved with the support of a city. This is true for non-farm employment in the city itself, as well as non-farm employment in the rural area.

However, urbanization of the interior is not necessarily most efficiently achieved by a thin distribution of small cities all over the area of the interior.

1.3. "Concentrated Dispersion"

The Second Indicative Plan 1999/2002 suggests a multi-sectoral approach for economic development. It is suggested that governmental interventions be concentrated in integrated programs and higher priority locations. This is a good approach, but it should not be translated into a focused intervention plan that is dispersed among too many places. Global spatial consideration is crucial for achieving a higher return on public investments (Rondinelli, 1983).

The achievement of agglomeration economies is required for a more efficient growth of the interior. A positive influence of the existence of an urban center and of its size on the ability of the rural area to develop non-farm activities has been clearly identified for the Northeast (Bar-El, 1990). An analysis of a French rural area by Schmitt and Henry (2000) also finds that "small urban places that have slow growing employment are associated with declining populations in nearby rural communities" while "medium size urban places ... have the strongest positive impacts on rural commune population change," and "large size urban places with faster fringe and core employment growth rates tend to increase rural population."

A natural change in the spatial structure is normally created by the process of "concentrated dispersion": the population and the economic activity are dispersed from the main metropolitan center, but they are not spread equally all over the state. The concentration of this dispersed population is achieved with the emergence of a new urban nucleus. The "Sustainable Economic Plan of Ceara" recognizes that the present situation is not acceptable, where the city of Fortaleza is 10 times bigger than the next biggest city in the state (Juazeiro do Norte). However, the policy measures that are being applied have not necessarily led to the creation of a more efficient spatial structure. The policy of the focused treatment of economic and social development problems, as it is implemented in the Projeto San Jose and in other programs, is an extremely efficient instrument in the fight against poverty: it supplies support to communities who express needs for infrastructures, education, etc. However, it also may lead to a too thinly spread development process, with no emergence of a significant concentration of development.

The conclusion is that an appropriate policy should on one hand provide answers to the needs of the poor communities and persons by supplying education, and the basic infrastructures of water, sewage, power and health services, but on the other hand it should support an efficient economic growth structure. This is achieved by focusing on the development of larger urban centers that can benefit from agglomeration economies, without neglecting the needs of smaller towns in the periphery of the centers, and without neglecting the economic and social needs of the entire population.

2. POLICY MEASURE: SPATIAL URBAN RESTRUCTURING

As explained above, the demographic and economic structural changes require state intervention for the reorganization of space in the interior. As an alternative to the growth pole concept, the concept that was adopted here is close to that of the Metropolitan-Based Regions (MBR). This concept was developed by McKenzie (1933) and Dickinson (1947), among others. It is employed as a methodological device for analyzing metropolitan change under conditions of rapid technological advance, changing communication structures, and continuing globalization. The MBR consists of two component parts: the metropolis or metropolitan part, as customarily defined, and a hinterland or surrounding non-metropolitan part. Metropolitan change is considered in terms of the whole MBR, where the system of interaction between the metropolitan zone and the surrounding non-metropolitan zone replaces the more familiar pattern of interaction among different parts of the metropolitan area itself (Parr, 1999; Bar-El & Parr, 2003).

The general idea is the stimulation of urban centers in the interior of Ceara that would serve as a basis for the economic development of their region and would attract some of the migrants from the migration flow to Fortaleza. The MBR argument is that the development of an urban center would result in the development of a whole region around this urban center. The region in our case is defined as all the municipalities that are close to the main urban center. In general terms, a close vicinity has been defined here as a commuting distance to the main urban center (about 40–60 km). A region would also include municipalities that have established strong economic relationships with the main urban center, even if the distance is somewhat greater than 60 km.

This program is intended to respond to the problem of inconsistency between the economic structure of the state and the demographic distribution of the population, leading to high levels of open and hidden unemployment, poverty, and inequality. The analysis of the economic and demographic data led to a plan of urban restructuring at two levels:

The first level is the support for the development of four major "secondary" urban centers (the primary being the metropolis). Those centers are actually regions, including a few municipalities, which follow the concept of a "MBR." Detailed plans for regional development of each of these centers are being developed by planning firms, following given directives: identification of the main economic basis, strengthening of the urban center with infrastructures and appropriate services, building a regional network, services to the rural hinterland, housing and social services, and educational networks, etc.

The second level is the support for the development of 14 "tertiary" urban centers. These are smaller urban locations which serve a smaller periphery of municipalities, and are intended to serve as centers mainly for local rural activities that need urban support such as marketing, production services, infrastructures for non-farm activities, education, etc.

A few of the expected effects of these policy measures are:

- *Increased agglomeration economies*: Increased capital productivity and competitiveness stimulate capital mobility and increases economic activity.
- *Increased labor mobility*: Wider occupational options stimulate the attraction of labor force from the rural area and mobility of workers between occupations, therefore increasing labor productivity.
- Increased support to the rural area through supply of services, demand for products, and therefore increased productivity of the rural sector.

3. "SECONDARY CENTERS," "TERTIARY CENTERS," AND THEIR REGIONS

Four Secondary Centers are identified. The following table shows the main central city or cities for each center, the municipalities that are defined as the Center region and the population of each municipality in 2000 (Table 1).

The first "secondary center" is Sobral, with the town of Sobral in its center, and a surrounding region of 16 municipalities. The urban population of Sobral itself reaches about 134,000 inhabitants, with an urbanization rate of 87%. The urban population of all other municipalities in the region is much smaller, and reaches at most less than 20,000. The total population in the region of Sobral is about 400,000 inhabitants.

The region of Limoiero do Norte has a total of about 250,000, with two main urban centers: Limoeiro do Norte and Russas, but also Morada Nova and Tabuleiro do Norte. The urbanization level of this region, including a total of eight municipalities is quite low (55%), but most of the urbanized municipalities in the region have a quite dense rural population: only a few municipalities can be considered as purely rural.

The so-called Crajubar region is the most populated and urbanized. It contains more than half a million inhabitants, with most of them concentrated in three highly urbanized municipalities, Crato, Juazeiro do Norte, and Barbalha, and the others in eight mostly rural municipalities.

The last region in this category is Iguatu, consisting of 10 municipalities with Iguatu as its center, but with a quite widely spread population over the region.

A total of 13 tertiary (or "regional") centers were identified and cover a total area of influence of 79 municipalities. The 13 Regional Centers are

Table 1. Secondary Centers and their Region, Regional Centers, and Other Municipalities: Population in 2000.

Centers		Municipality	Total Population	Urban	Rural	Urbanization Rate
Four secondary centers						
Sobral						
	Main urban center	Sobral	155,120	134,371	20,749	0.87
	Region	Alcântaras	9,548	2,759	6,789	0.29
		Cariré	18,645	5,448	13,197	0.29
		Coreaú	19,974	11,262	8,712	0.56
		Forquilha	17,498	11,625	5,873	0.66
		Groaíras	8,736	5,582	3,154	0.64
		Massapê	29,524	19,127	10,397	0.65
		Meruoca	11,340	5,634	5,706	0.50
		Miraíma	11,413	4,772	6,641	0.42
		Moraújo	7,018	3,324	3,694	0.47
		Morrinhos	17,921	7,736	10,185	0.43
		Pacujá	5,644	3,265	2,379	0.58
		Reriutaba	21,211	9,728	11,483	0.46
		Santana do Acaraú	26,195	12,452	13,743	0.48
		Senador Sá	5,579	3,800	1,779	0.68
		Uruoca	11,474	6,116	5,358	0.53
		Varjota	16,598	13,481	3,117	0.81
Sobral Total			393,438	260,482	132,956	0.66
Limoeiro Do Norte						
	Main urban centers	Limoeiro do Norte	49,580	28,174	21,406	0.57
		Russas	57,290	35,292	21,998	0.62
	Region	Alto Santo	15,392	5,445	9,947	0.35
		Ibicuitinga	9,428	4,388	5,040	0.47
		Morada Nova	64,394	33,869	30,525	0.53
		Quixeré	16,856	9,850	7,006	0.58
		São João do Jaguaribe	8,639	2,737	5,902	0.32
		Tabuleiro do Norte	27,098	15,850	11,248	0.58
Limoeiro do Norte, total			248,677	135,605	113,072	0.55
Crajubar						
	Main urban centers	Crato	104,377	83,744	20,633	0.80
		Juazeiro do Norte	211,858	201,950	9,908	0.95
		Barbalha	46,997	30,657	16,340	0.65
	Region	Aurora	25,442	10,026	15,416	0.39
		Caririaçu	25,732	10,625	15,107	0.41
		Farias Brito	20,325	8,736	11,589	0.43
		Granjeiro	5,298	1,231	4,067	0.23

Table 1. (*Continued*)

Centers	Municipality	Total Population	Urban	Rural	Urbanization Rate
	Jardim	26,463	7,352	19,111	0.28
	Missão Velha	32,204	12,769	19,435	0.40
	Nova Olinda	12,079	6,391	5,688	0.53
	Santana do Cariri	16,836	8,185	8,651	0.49
Crajubar total		527,611	381,666	145,945	0.72
Iguatu					
Main urban center	Iguatu	85,737	62,489	23,248	0.73
Region	Acopiara	47,103	22,212	24,891	0.47
	Cariús	18,449	7,166	11,283	0.39
	Cedro	24,065	13,506	10,559	0.56
	Icó	62,494	26,035	36,459	0.42
	Jucás	22,613	11,840	10,773	0.52
	Lavras da Mangabeira	31,102	16,658	14,444	0.54
	Orós	21,944	15,722	6,222	0.72
	Quixelô	15,594	4,166	11,428	0.27
	Várzea Alegre	34,804	19,252	15,552	0.55
Iguatu total		363,905	199,046	164,859	0.55
Total of 4 secondary centers		1,533,631	976,799	556,832	0.64
13 regional centers					
14 main urban centers		767,523	462,854	304,669	0.60
65 regional municipalities		1,097,016	509,260	587,756	0.46
Total of 13 regional centers		1,986,780	1,020,128	966,652	0.51
Other municipalities					
Total of 46 other municipalities		922,362	434,942	487,420	0.47

represented by 14 central municipalities (one of the center includes two main urban municipalities): Acaraú, Aracati, Baturité, Brejo Santo, Camocim, Campos Sales, Canindé, Crateús, Itapipoca, Jaguaribe, Quixadá and Quixeramobim, Tauá, Tianguá. Those have a total population of close to 800,000 inhabitants, with a rate of urbanization of 60%. They are surrounded by 65 municipalities with more than a million inhabitants and a rate of urbanization of 46%.

The last 49 municipalities that do not fall into the area of influence of any tertiary center or secondary city are mostly isolated municipalities, with a total population of about 900,000 inhabitants, of which 47% are urban. Those should be added to the area of influence of the nearest tertiary center or given a special attention by the public sector.

4. A GLOBAL TYPOLOGY: URBAN CENTERS AND THEIR REGIONS

In order to provide a general picture of the situation of the various urban centers and of their regions, we use the Index of Municipal Development that has been developed by IPLANCE (see Governo do Estado do Ceara, 2004). As explained there, the index is based on 27 main variables, in 4 groups representing variables in the fields of agriculture, demography and economics, infrastructure support, and social situation (see there details of the specific variables).

An index for each of the 4 groups and for all groups together is calculated there. The 184 municipalities of Ceara are then ranked according to the value of the index for each group and for the total. The ranking has a value of 1 for the best municipality in the group, and 184 for the worst.

The following table presents simple averages of the ranking (as problematic as such a simplification may be) for groups of municipalities as defined in above, distinguishing between the main urban centers and their regions. The 184 municipalities are therefore classified into the main urban center of Fortaleza and its region, the main secondary urban centers and their regions, the main Regional Centers and their regions, and other municipalities that are not included into any of those regions (Table 2).

The average rank is 92.5 for the total of all municipalities (equal to the average of the best rank (1) with the worst rank (184)). Looking at the global index, we see that:

1. The index of municipal development is best for the main centers, beginning with Fortaleza, followed by the Secondary Centers, and then the Regional Centers. The urban centers at the higher level of hierarchy certainly enjoy better levels of development.
2. The surrounding regions always have a lower level of development. However, the level of development of municipalities in the regions of Secondary and Regional Centers is lower than that of municipalities around the metropolitan center of Fortaleza.
3. Still, there are no significant differences between the regions around the Secondary Centers, the Regional Centers, or the municipalities that are not included in any of those regions. This apparently indicates a lack of influence today of the existing centers on their regions or a lack of integration between the urban centers and the rural hinterland.

A general conclusion at this stage is therefore that the growth of urban centers clearly contributes to the development index of their municipalities

Table 2. Average Ranking of Municipalities in the Index of Municipal Development, by Groups (Simple Averages by Municipality, 1 is Best Rank, 184 is Last).

Region	Global Index	Group 1: Agricultural Index	Group 2: Demographic and Economic Index	Group 3: Support Infrastructure Index	Group 4: Social Index
Total	93	93	93	93	93
RMF total: 13 mun.					
Center: 1 mun.	1	23	1	1	3
Region: 12 mun.	50	80	20	40	109
SC total: 46 mun.					
Centers: 7 mun.	11	55	20	23	15
Region: 39 mun.	104	95	101	99	101
RC total: 79 mun.					
Centers: 14 mun.	51	65	63	59	59
Regions: 65 mun.	91	93	99	103	84
Others total: 46 mun.	117	105	113	109	112
Secondary centers					
Sobral total					
Sobral	6	133	7	3	4
Sobral region: 16 mun.	118	144	92	80	108
Limoeiro-Russas total					
Limoeiro do Norte	10	21	33	7	35
Russas	45	131	49	30	45
Region: 6 mun.	90	96	66	86	100
Crajubar total					
Crato	2	15	11	14	1
Juazeiro do Norte	8	66	5	8	15
Barbalha	5	9	12	98	2
Region: 8 mun.	112	47	130	141	115
Iguatu total					
Iguatu	4	10	22	2	5
Region: 9 mun.	83	50	116	104	78

(higher level centers have better ranks), but the benefits of urban growth in the interior are not yet shared with the surrounding more rural regions. An effort for a better regional integration is needed.

Another interesting conclusion from the data is that the social index (group four) is generally equal, on average, in all groups of municipalities around the urban centers, including Fortaleza. The urban centers themselves are better ranked, but it seems that the policy of social support to less urbanized municipalities actually compensates for the worse economic and demographical conditions there. This is in terms of the various variables that represent the social level of development: schooling, water supply, health services, etc.

5. DEMOGRAPHIC SPATIAL PATTERNS

The population of Ceara reached about 7.4 million inhabitants in 2000, growing at an annual rate of about 1.8% in the previous 30 years. All the population growth is concentrated in the urban sector, while the population of the rural sector shows a clear long-term trend of decline.

However, an analysis of the spatial patterns of the demographic growth shows a few important characteristics (see Table 3 at the end of this section):

1. There is a constant very well-known trend of concentration of the population in the Metropolitan Region of Fortaleza (RMF). However, this trend has lost some of its strength in recent years, although it still exists. During the period of 1970–1991, the RMF grew at an annual rate of 3.8% compared with about 1% in the other regions; in the last decade, the rate of growth declined to 2.4% in the RMF, while that of other regions increased: the Secondary Centers together with their regions grew in the last decade at a higher rate of 1.5%, and the Regional Centers with their regions reached 1.3%. Other isolated municipalities still keep a low rate of growth of about 1% a year. Therefore, the process of concentration is continuing, although at a slower pace.
2. The migration annual rate, evaluated on the basis of the assumption that the natural growth rate is more or less equal in the various regions, also shows a continuing attraction of the RMF, although at a declining rate: 0.7% in the last decade, compared with 2.0% in the previous two decades. The share of the region around Fortaleza in the attraction of migrants increases constantly, compared with the attraction of Fortaleza itself.
3. The Secondary Centers and the Regional Centers do not yet show any significant attraction of migrants, but the net migration balance from them is clearly decreasing. The municipalities of the Secondary Centers themselves even show in the last decade a positive balance of migration. This is true for each of the centers. The other isolated municipalities continue with a steady negative migration balance for all years. As a consequence, we can identify a stabilization trend of the share of the RMF in the total population, and of the share of the Secondary and Regional Centers together with a steady slow decline in the share of the isolated municipalities.

4. The process of urbanization is steady and clear in all regions. We can identify a trend of convergence of the urbanization rate: a more rapid process of urbanization in more rural areas, leading to greater equality between the urbanization rates over the state. Greatest annual growth of the urbanization rate is achieved in the most isolated municipalities ("other"), indicating a tendency of spatial re-organization to confront the declining ability of agriculture to provide employment.

We conclude here that there is a natural tendency of consolidation of a spatial restructuring of demographic distribution in Ceara. This tendency is a natural answer to the decreasing weight of agriculture in the economy and the need for the development of non-farm employment. However, such structural changes cannot happen only on the basis of a free economy. Urbanization processes require quite heavy involvement of the public sector, in terms of building infrastructures, support services, etc. The intensification of these trends in the last decade can probably be at least partly attributed to the public policy of support for urban development (the PROURB program). Still, the growth and urbanization of most municipalities does not indicate any formation of new development centers, perhaps as a result of the prevailing policy of spreading undifferentiated support to a large number of urban places. The need to stimulate agglomeration economies requires heavier support of the public sector in the development and consolidation of bigger urban centers.

An evaluation of expected trends in the future until 2020, based on projections of the IBGE for 2010, leads to the conclusion that the present trends are not sufficient for the solution of the problem of demographic concentration. The following three tables are the results of the simulations of three alternative scenarios, as elaborated by Alex Araujo in his position as president of IPLANCE and later as Secretary of Local and Regional Development. The first is the "business as usual" scenario, following the existing trends, on the basis of the IBGE projections for each municipality. The second assumes the implementation of a policy of "migration deviation" from Fortaleza. The third assumes, in addition, a policy of reinforcement of the urbanization process (see Tables 3–7).

The population of Ceara is expected to reach about 10 million inhabitants in 2020, meaning an annual growth rate of 1.55%. The "business as usual" scenario leads to an increase in the urbanization rate up to 81% from the present rate of 72%. However, the share of the RMF in total population is expected to grow until almost half of the total population, against a decreasing weight for both the Secondary Centers and the Regional Centers.

Table 3. Demographic Spatial Patterns.

Region	Population in 2000	Population Density in 2000	Annual Population Growth from 1970 to 1991			Annual Population Growth from 1991 to 2000			Distribution of Population			Annual Evaluated Migration Rate		Urbanization Rate			Annual Change of Urbanization Rate	
			Total	Urban	Rural	Total	Urban	Rural	1970	1991	2000	1970–1991	1991–2000	1970	1991	2000	1970–1991	1991–2000
Total	7,418,476	51	1.8%	4.1%	−0.7%	1.7%	2.7%	−0.5%	100%	100%	100%	0.0%	0.0%	0.41	0.65	0.72	1.9%	1.0%
RMF total: 13 mun.	2,975,703	598	3.8%	4.6%	−3.4%	2.4%	2.5%	0.7%	25%	38%	40%	2.0%	0.7%	0.81	0.96	0.97	0.6%	0.1%
Center: 1 mun.	2,138,234	6,814	3.5%	3.7%	−100.0%	2.1%	2.1%	0.0%	20%	28%	29%	1.7%	0.4%	0.96	1.00	1.00	0.1%	0.0%
Region: 12 mun.	837,469	180	4.9%	10.9%	−2.7%	3.2%	3.5%	0.7%	5%	10%	11%	3.0%	1.4%	0.26	0.85	0.88	4.1%	0.4%
SC total: 46 mun.	1,533,631	44	1.1%	3.3%	−0.8%	1.5%	2.6%	−0.3%	25%	21%	21%	−0.7%	−0.3%	0.37	0.57	0.64	1.9%	1.2%
Centers: 7 mun.	710,959	97	1.5%	3.2%	−1.9%	2.0%	2.4%	0.6%	10%	9%	10%	−0.3%	0.3%	0.56	0.79	0.81	1.2%	0.3%
Region: 39 mun.	822,672	30	0.7%	3.4%	−0.5%	1.0%	3.0%	−0.6%	15%	12%	11%	−1.1%	−0.7%	0.23	0.41	0.49	2.5%	2.0%
RC total: 79 mun.	1,986,780	32	0.7%	3.6%	−0.7%	1.3%	3.2%	−0.4%	35%	28%	27%	−1.1%	−0.4%	0.24	0.44	0.51	2.6%	1.9%
Centers: 14 mun.	767,523	32	0.1%	3.3%	−1.9%	0.9%	2.6%	−1.2%	16%	11%	10%	−1.7%	−0.8%	0.27	0.52	0.60	2.8%	1.7%
Regions: 65 mun.	1,097,016	32	0.9%	3.8%	−0.3%	1.5%	3.7%	−0.1%	18%	15%	15%	−0.9%	−0.2%	0.21	0.38	0.46	2.6%	2.1%
Others total: 46 mun.	922,362	21	1.1%	4.2%	0.0%	1.0%	3.7%	−1.0%	15%	13%	12%	−0.7%	−0.7%	0.20	0.37	0.47	2.9%	2.8%
Secondary centers																		
Sobral total	393,438	41	1.0%	3.1%	−1.0%	1.9%	3.2%	−0.4%	6%	5%	5%	−0.8%	0.1%	0.38	0.59	0.66	1.9%	1.3%
Sobral	155,120	73	1.1%	2.6%	−2.7%	2.2%	2.9%	−1.4%	2%	2%	2%	−0.7%	0.5%	0.59	0.81	0.87	1.3%	0.7%
Sobral region: 16 mun.	238,318	32	0.9%	3.8%	−0.5%	1.6%	3.6%	−0.1%	4%	3%	3%	−0.9%	−0.1%	0.25	0.45	0.53	2.5%	1.9%
Limoeiro-Russas total	248,677	29	1.3%	5.1%	−0.6%	1.6%	2.9%	0.2%	4%	3%	3%	−0.5%	−0.1%	0.23	0.49	0.55	3.0%	1.3%
Limoeiro do Norte	49,580	64	2.3%	6.4%	−0.2%	1.9%	2.1%	1.7%	1%	1%	1%	0.5%	0.2%	0.25	0.56	0.57	2.8%	0.2%
Russas	57,290	35	1.5%	4.2%	−0.8%	2.3%	3.0%	1.3%	1%	1%	1%	−0.3%	0.6%	0.33	0.58	0.62	2.1%	0.7%
Region: 6 mun.	141,807	23	1.0%	5.1%	−0.7%	1.1%	3.1%	−0.6%	2%	2%	2%	−0.8%	−0.6%	0.19	0.43	0.51	3.4%	2.0%
Crajubar total	527,611	87	1.4%	3.1%	−1.0%	1.8%	2.3%	0.4%	8%	7%	7%	−0.4%	0.1%	0.48	0.69	0.72	1.4%	0.6%
Crato	104,377	93	1.2%	2.5%	−1.7%	1.6%	2.0%	0.2%	2%	1%	1%	−0.6%	−0.1%	0.59	0.78	0.80	1.0%	0.4%
Juazeiro do Norte	211,858	900	2.9%	3.5%	−2.7%	2.2%	2.3%	1.5%	2%	3%	3%	1.0%	0.5%	0.84	0.95	0.95	0.4%	0.0%
Barbalha	46,997	104	2.0%	4.5%	−0.5%	2.3%	2.6%	1.6%	1%	1%	1%	0.2%	0.5%	0.38	0.63	0.65	1.8%	0.3%
Region: 8 mun.	164,379	38	0.0%	2.2%	−0.8%	1.2%	2.9%	0.2%	3%	2%	2%	−1.7%	−0.5%	0.22	0.34	0.40	2.1%	1.7%
Iguatu total	363,905	33	0.6%	2.8%	−0.7%	0.5%	2.3%	−1.2%	7%	5%	5%	−1.2%	−1.2%	0.30	0.47	0.55	2.0%	1.7%
Iguatu	85,737	82	0.0%	2.5%	−3.1%	1.4%	1.8%	0.4%	2%	1%	1%	−1.8%	−0.3%	0.42	0.70	0.73	1.8%	0.4%
Region: 9 mun.	278,168	28	0.8%	3.0%	−0.2%	0.3%	2.5%	−1.4%	5%	4%	4%	−1.0%	−1.4%	0.26	0.40	0.49	2.2%	2.2%

Table 4. Cenário Tendencial – Projeções do IBGE, com Taxa de Urbanização Estimada.

Espaços	Pop. 2000	Prop.	Pop. 2020	Prop.	Cresc.	Pop. Urbana	Pop. Rural	Tx Urban
Região Metrop. Fortaleza	2,975,703	40.11%	4,909,710	48.61%	2.54%	4,749,991	159,719	96.75%
Centros Secundários	1,533,631	20.67%	1,855,110	18.37%	0.96%	1,353,056	502,054	72.94%
A21: J. do Norte, Crato e Barbalha	527,611	7.11%	728,183	7.21%	1.62%	561,037	167,151	77.05%
A22: Sobral	393,438	5.30%	494,932	4.90%	1.15%	370,218	124,714	74.80%
A23: L. do Norte, M. Nova e Russas	248,677	3.35%	310,743	3.08%	1.12%	203,031	107,712	65.34%
A24: Iguatu	363,905	4.91%	321,247	3.18%	−0.62%	218,771	102,476	68.10%
Centros Regionais	1,986,780	26.78%	2,355,355	23.32%	0.85%	1,484,843	870,513	63.04%
AR1: Acaraú	160,021	2.16%	333,176	3.30%	3.73%	160,744	172,432	48.25%
AR2: Aracati	117,697	1.59%	183,880	1.82%	2.26%	137,199	46,681	74.61%
AR3: Baturité	210,218	2.83%	267,336	2.65%	1.21%	150,575	116,761	56.32%
AR4: Brejo Santo	166,107	2.24%	153,623	1.52%	−0.39%	89,573	64,055	58.31%
AR5: Camocim	126,447	1.70%	139,515	1.38%	0.49%	103,312	36,203	74.05%
AR6: Campos Sales	68,086	0.92%	62,153	0.62%	−0.45%	41,441	20,712	66.68%
AR7: Canindé	116,538	1.57%	146,517	1.45%	1.15%	100,332	46,185	68.48%
AR8: Cratéus	82,052	1.11%	63,757	0.63%	−1.25%	47,063	16,694	73.82%
AR9: Itapipoca	232,562	3.13%	278,511	2.76%	0.91%	183,547	94,964	65.90%
AR10: Jaguaribe	90,120	1.21%	74,421	0.74%	−0.95%	48,337	26,084	64.95%
AR11: Quixadá e Quixeramobim	250,191	3.37%	217,783	2.16%	−0.69%	146,228	71,555	67.14%
AR12: Tauá	59,477	0.80%	48,422	0.48%	−1.02%	31,080	17,342	64.19%
AR13: Tianguá	307,264	4.14%	386,257	3.82%	1.15%	245,411	140,846	63.54%
Outros municípios	922,362	12.43%	979,268	9.70%	0.30%	607,072	372,196	61.99%
Ceará total	7,418,476	100.00%	10,099,444	100.00%	1.55%	8,194,962	1,904,482	81.14%

Notas: (a) a população total de 2020 é a projetada pelo IBGE; (b) a taxa de crescimento está anualizada.

Table 5. Cenário Migração Desviada – 75% da Migração Interna Para a RMF é Desviada.

Espaços	Pop. 2000	Prop.	Pop. 2020	Prop.	Cresc.	Pop. Urbana	Pop. Rural	Tx Urban
Região Metrop. Fortaleza	2,975,703	40.11%	4,265,748	42.24%	1.82%	4,106,029	159,719	96.26%
Centros Secundários	1,533,631	20.67%	2,305,883	22.83%	2.06%	1,803,829	502,054	78.23%
A21: J. do Norte, Crato e Barbalha	527,611	7.11%	905,130	8.96%	2.74%	737,980	167,151	81.53%
A22: Sobral	393,438	5.30%	615,195	6.09%	2.26%	490,481	124,714	79.73%
A23: L. do Norte, M. Nova e Russas	248,677	3.35%	386,250	3.82%	2.23%	278,538	107,712	72.11%
A24: Iguatu	363,905	4.91%	399,307	3.95%	0.47%	296,830	102,476	74.34%
Centros Regionais	1,986,780	26.78%	2,548,545	25.23%	1.25%	1,678,032	870,513	65.84%
AR1: Acaraú	160,021	2.16%	360,503	3.57%	4.14%	188,071	172,432	52.17%
AR2: Aracati	117,697	1.59%	198,962	1.97%	2.66%	152,281	46,681	76.54%
AR3: Baturité	210,218	2.83%	289,263	2.86%	1.61%	172,502	116,761	59.64%
AR4: Brejo Santo	166,107	2.24%	166,229	1.65%	0.00%	102,174	64,055	61.47%
AR5: Camocim	126,447	1.70%	150,958	1.49%	0.89%	114,755	36,203	76.02%
AR6: Campos Sales	68,086	0.92%	67,251	0.67%	−0.06%	46,539	20,712	69.20%
AR7: Canindé	116,538	1.57%	158,534	1.57%	1.55%	112,350	46,185	70.87%
AR8: Cratéus	82,052	1.11%	68,986	0.68%	−0.86%	52,293	16,694	75.80%
AR9: Itapipoca	232,562	3.13%	301,355	2.98%	1.30%	206,391	94,964	68.49%
AR10: Jaguaribe	90,120	1.21%	80,525	0.80%	−0.56%	54,441	26,084	67.61%
AR11: Quixadá e Quixeramobim	250,191	3.37%	235,646	2.33%	−0.30%	164,090	71,555	69.63%
AR12: Tauá	59,477	0.80%	52,394	0.52%	−0.63%	35,051	17,342	66.90%
AR13: Tianguá	307,264	4.14%	417,938	4.14%	1.55%	277,092	140,846	66.30%
Outros municípios	922,362	12.43%	979,268	9.70%	0.30%	607,072	372,196	61.99%
Ceará total	7,418,476	100.00%	10,099,444	100.00%	1.55%	8,194,962	1,904,482	81.14%

Notas: (a) a população total de 2020 é a projetada pelo IBGE; (b) a taxa de crescimento está anualizada.

Table 6. Cenário Urbanização – 75% da Migração Interna Para a RMF é Desviada, 90% de Taxa de Urbanização.

Espaços	Pop. 2000	Prop.	Pop. 2020	Prop.	Cresc.	Pop. Urbana	Pop. Rural	Tx Urban
Região Metrop. Fortaleza	2,975,703	40.11%	4,265,748	42.24%	1.82%	4,106,029	159,719	96.26%
Centros Secundários	1,533,631	20.67%	2,674,657	26.48%	2.82%	2,430,005	244,652	90.85%
A21: J. do Norte, Crato e Barbalha	527,611	7.11%	1,065,226	10.55%	3.58%	983,773	81,453	92.35%
A22: Sobral	393,438	5.30%	718,315	7.11%	3.06%	657,541	60,774	91.54%
A23: L. do Norte, M. Nova e Russas	248,677	3.35%	435,915	4.32%	2.85%	383,427	52,488	87.96%
A24: Iguatu	363,905	4.91%	455,202	4.51%	1.13%	405,265	49,937	89.03%
Centros Regionais	1,986,780	26.78%	2,370,596	23.47%	0.89%	1,946,393	424,203	82.11%
AR1: Acaraú	160,021	2.16%	310,058	3.07%	3.36%	226,032	84,026	72.90%
AR2: Aracati	117,697	1.59%	195,980	1.94%	2.58%	173,232	22,748	88.39%
AR3: Baturité	210,218	2.83%	259,860	2.57%	1.07%	202,962	56,898	78.10%
AR4: Brejo Santo	166,107	2.24%	150,892	1.49%	−0.48%	119,678	31,214	79.31%
AR5: Camocim	126,447	1.70%	148,293	1.47%	0.80%	130,651	17,642	88.10%
AR6: Campos Sales	68,086	0.92%	63,714	0.63%	−0.33%	53,621	10,093	84.16%
AR7: Canindé	116,538	1.57%	151,550	1.50%	1.32%	129,044	22,506	85.15%
AR8: Cratéus	82,052	1.11%	67,692	0.67%	−0.96%	59,557	8,135	87.98%
AR9: Itapipoca	232,562	3.13%	284,400	2.82%	1.01%	238,124	46,276	83.73%
AR10: Jaguaribe	90,120	1.21%	75,631	0.75%	−0.87%	62,920	12,711	83.19%
AR11: Quixadá e Quixeramobim	250,191	3.37%	223,773	2.22%	−0.56%	188,904	34,869	84.42%
AR12: Tauá	59,477	0.80%	49,019	0.49%	−0.96%	40,568	8,451	82.76%
AR13: Tianguá	307,264	4.14%	389,735	3.86%	1.20%	321,101	68,634	82.39%
Outros municípios	922,362	12.43%	788,444	7.81%	−0.78%	607,072	181,372	77.00%
Ceará total	7,418,476	100.00%	10,099,445	100.00%	1.55%	9,089,499	1,009,944	90.00%

Notas: (a) a população total de 2020 é a projetada pelo IBGE; (b) a taxa de crescimento está anualizada.

Table 7. Economic Characteristics.

Region	Agricultural Conditions				PIB p/c 1998	PIB by Sectors 1998 (%)			Employment by Sector 1991 (%)			Energy Consumption p/c, Average MPH 1995–1999		Types of Industrial Firms 1999 (%)		Income p/c, 1995 (Simple Averages)
	Regular annual rainfall mm.(simple averages)	Inverse of salinity index	Rural energy p/c rural (MPH average 1995–1999)	Rural population density		Agriculture	Industry	Services	Agriculture	Industry	Services	In industry	In commerce	Traditional (textile, clothing, food)	Local consumption and processing of local raw materials	
Total	949	1.23	0.14	14	2,691	6%	40%	54%	33%	18%	46%	0.19	0.11	59%	23%	1,212
RMF total: 13 mun.	1,198	1.01	0.48	21	4,159	1%	50%	49%	5%	26%	66%	0.38	0.23	60%	17%	2,569
Center: 1 mun.	1,338	1.06	0.00	0	3,515	0%	36%	64%	2%	25%	70%	0.25	0.30	63%	15%	3,697
Region: 12 mun.	1,187	1.01	0.40	22	5,875	3%	72%	26%	17%	30%	52%	0.70	0.06	49%	27%	2,475
SC total: 46 mun.	915	1.35	0.18	16	2,146	8%	41%	51%	42%	17%	40%	0.14	0.05	54%	30%	1,116
Centers: 7 mun.	911	2.56	0.45	18	3,085	4%	56%	40%	21%	22%	56%	0.29	0.09	55%	27%	1,874
Regions: 39 mun.	915	1.14	0.10	15	1,356	16%	12%	73%	60%	12%	27%	0.02	0.02	51%	39%	980
RC total: 79 mun.	979	1.27	0.10	16	1,463	18%	11%	71%	56%	11%	32%	0.03	0.03	61%	28%	1,107
Centers: 14 mun.	887	0.95	0.10	13	1,545	17%	13%	70%	48%	13%	38%	0.03	0.04	56%	29%	1,210
Regions: 65 mun.	994	1.38	0.10	17	1,411	19%	9%	72%	61%	10%	28%	0.03	0.02	67%	24%	1,098
Others total: 46 mun.	861	1.10	0.08	11	1,473	17%	14%	69%	61%	11%	27%	0.03	0.02	56%	34%	1,105
Secondary centers																
Sobral total	975	0.81	0.08	14	3,350	4%	64%	32%	38%	23%	38%	0.37	0.05	59%	25%	1,125
Sobral	822	0.70	0.20	10	6,729	1%	81%	18%	16%	26%	56%	0.94	0.10	61%	19%	3,877
Sobral region: 16 mun.	985	0.82	0.05	15	1,229	13%	5%	82%	51%	21%	26%	0.01	0.02	57%	37%	953
Limoeiro-Russas total	814	0.49	0.50	13	1,990	15%	30%	55%	43%	17%	38%	0.08	0.04	42%	47%	1,220
Limoeiro do Norte	721	0.57	1.35	28	2,473	18%	36%	46%	34%	19%	46%	0.13	0.06	55%	30%	1,450
Russas	858	0.23	0.40	14	1,896	9%	32%	59%	29%	27%	43%	0.10	0.05	33%	60%	1,264
Region: 6 mun.	822	0.53	0.27	11	1,862	16%	26%	57%	52%	13%	34%	0.06	0.03	41%	46%	1,174
Crajubar total	977	2.84	0.11	24	1,766	6%	31%	63%	33%	18%	48%	0.08	0.07	57%	25%	1,116
Crato	1,091	5.30	0.16	18	1,890	4%	36%	59%	24%	18%	55%	0.08	0.09	49%	36%	1,550
Juazeiro do Norte	925	3.50	0.25	42	1,766	1%	24%	76%	9%	23%	66%	0.06	0.10	59%	20%	1,314
Barbalha	1,153	5.79	0.25	36	3,574	6%	67%	27%	29%	28%	41%	0.44	0.05	61%	20%	2,448
Region: 8 mun.	947	2.08	0.07	23	1,166	19%	6%	75%	69%	8%	22%	0.01	0.02	47%	42%	870
Iguatu total	830	1.33	0.12	15	1,504	14%	11%	74%	58%	9%	33%	0.02	0.04	55%	31%	1,019
Iguatu	807	1.85	0.37	22	2,125	12%	15%	73%	34%	13%	52%	0.04	0.09	54%	27%	1,211
Region: 9 mun.	833	1.27	0.08	14	1,319	15%	10%	75%	65%	7%	27%	0.02	0.03	56%	34%	998

The expected trends also will lead to the continuation of the decrease of the relative weight of isolated ("other") municipalities in the total population, from 12% today to less than 10% in 2020.

The scenario of migration deviation assumes that a policy is adopted to stimulate a diversion of 75% of the expected migrants to the RMF toward the Secondary Centers (70% of them) and the Regional Centers (30%). Many of those "diverted" migrants may actually be potential migrants from the Secondary Centers who decide finally to stay in their regions as a consequence of a policy for the development of those regions. Such a policy would finally lead to a much smaller increase in the weight of the RMF and an increase in the weight of the Secondary Centers up to 23% of total population. The scenario of a more rapid urbanization process would lead to a more significant increase in the weight of those centers, up to more than 26% of total population.

6. ECONOMIC CHARACTERISTICS

A few indicators of the economic characteristics in each type of region are displayed in Table 7 (above).

The basic agricultural conditions are measured in terms of regular annual rainfall (calculated by IBGE as a long-term average) and the inverse salinity indicator as developed by IPECE (Governo do Estado do Ceara, 2004). Data for regions are calculated as simple averages for all municipalities in the region. The RMF enjoys a good rainfall average, although the salinity index average is not too good. A much better combination is achieved mostly in the regions of the Regional Centers, with a good average rainfall and a good salinity index (high inverse value). It should also be indicated that the 65 municipalities that form the regions around the Regional Centers show better conditions than those of the 14 municipalities of the centers themselves. The Secondary Centers are on the whole close to the state average, with best conditions at the Crajubar region. However, most of these regions benefit from their proximity to irrigation projects. The "other" isolated municipalities suffer mostly with a low rainfall average and a bad salinity index.

Those isolated municipalities also have the lowest average rural density, calculated as the rural population for each square kilometer of the municipality. This is probably a result of the bad agricultural conditions, but at the same time this low population density imposes serious constraints on the ability to develop services and non-farm economic activities. The indicator of rural energy per capita of rural population is also low, testifying a low level of economic activity. The other groups of regions show better achievements. It is interesting to show that the relatively high population density of the municipalities around Fortaleza and their proximity to a major urban center lead to a major level of economic activity there, as indicated by the consumption of rural energy per rural inhabitant. Proximity to a main urban center permits the relocation of some industrial activity from the city to the rural area, at lower land costs, thus providing employment to the rural workers as well as to the commuting city workers. As can be seen through the share of agriculture in the Gross Internal Product (Produto Interno Bruto: PIB) and in employment, most of this rural activity is not agricultural but industrial. The prevailing structure of the Secondary Centers does not yet offer to the rural inhabitants the benefits of proximity to a city. The rural use of energy per capita is quite high within the municipalities where the Secondary Centers are located, but is low in the region around those municipalities. The Regional Centers do not even reach this level: the energy use per capita is low even in the municipalities of the centers.

The data on the distribution of the PIB and of employment by economic sectors in each group of regions give an indication about the potential for regional development that can emanate from the strengthening of urban centers. The municipalities around Fortaleza have a much greater share of industry in their economy than Fortaleza itself. The metropolitan city concentrates mainly in service activities, while most of the industrial activity is "exported" to the neighboring region. This does not happen yet in the regions of the Secondary Centers: most of the industrial activity concentrates in the urban centers themselves, while the neighboring regions are characterized by high levels of employment in services (and agriculture), probably implying high levels of disguised unemployment. A similar picture is shown by the data on energy per capita used in industry and in commerce in each group of regions. A consolidation of strong urban centers in those regions would permit greater specialization by the main cities in services, while industrial activity is located mostly in the surrounding region.

Regarding the type of industrial activity, it is important to notice that in comparative terms the main centers concentrate more on textile and other traditional activities while the surrounding regions show a relatively high share of local oriented industry: production for local consumption and processing of local raw materials.

The result of such patterns of economic development is the creation of higher levels of income in main urban centers and in their surrounding regions. The leading case is that of the RMF, where Fortaleza shows the highest level of income per capita, and its region benefits from the proximity to the big center: the average income level per capita, although lower than that of Fortaleza, is higher than the average of any group of regions. The regions around the Secondary Centers and the Regional Centers have not yet reached this level.

Concluding this section, we can say that the development of urban centers mostly in Secondary Cities can provide a substantive potential for the economic growth of the whole region around them, not only by facilitating agricultural development, but mostly by permitting industrial growth.

7. SUPPORTING INFRASTRUCTURES

The ability of a region to develop depends to a large extent upon the infrastructures that support the economic activity and the needs of the population. Some basic measures of infrastructures are presented in the following table for groups of regions.

Proximity to Fortaleza or to a Secondary Center is not by itself a measure of infrastructure, but it indicates the accessibility of each region to the infrastructures and services of the main urban centers, and therefore clearly influences the potential and nature of economic development in a region. Two indicators are used here: the distance to Fortaleza and the distance to the closest Secondary Center.

The Secondary Centers themselves have an average low level of proximity to Fortaleza (simple averages by municipality), but this actually represents two types of centers: Sobral and Limeiro which are quite close to the Metropolitan center (about 200–250 km), and Crajubar and Iguatu which are located at a significant distance (400–530 km). Those centers can have a much lower access to the infrastructures, services, and market of the RMF, and therefore would have to develop a more independent type of economic growth.

The consolidation of a new spatial distribution, with the Secondary Centers as new strong urban centers, would improve accessibility from the interior to urban amenities to a large extent. In addition to the 46 municipalities of the Secondary Centers themselves that would enjoy a distance of less than 50 km on average from the main urban center, the 79 municipalities of the Regional Centers would enjoy an average distance of about 100 km from a Secondary Center, instead of the average of about 250 km from Fortaleza. Even the 46 so-called isolated ("other") municipalities would enjoy more or less the same distance from the Secondary Centers, against an average distance of about 300 km from Fortaleza. As a matter of fact, only three municipalities would be at a distance of more than 200 km from any main urban location

(Secondary Center or RMF): Novo Oriente with 26,000 inhabitants, Parambu with 32,000, and Quiterianópolis with 18,000. Only 14 municipalities would be at a distance of more than 150 km.

Accessibility to main urban centers is also a function of the density of roads in the municipalities, as measured by the road length per square km of the area of the municipality. A typical pattern of a road system would be represented by a high road density in the main urban center, and a lower density in its surrounding region, since the roads from each region are expected to all lead to the main urban center. This is actually the picture in the RMF, where the road density in the municipality of Fortaleza is about 50% greater than that of the other municipalities of the RMF. The picture shown in the regions of the Secondary Centers does not fit this pattern: the density of roads is on average the same in the centers as in the surrounding region (0.52). In each region separately, we can even see that in a few cases the road density in the municipality of the Secondary Center is less than that of other municipalities in the region. The only region that shows the pattern of a main urban center for a hinterland region is Iguatu, where the road density of the municipality of Iguatu is greater than the average road density in the region.

Concluding the analysis of distances and accessibility, we can say that the spatial distribution of the population as suggested in Secondary and Regional Centers certainly presents a strong potential for the reduction of the isolation effect and for the increase of accessibility to urban amenities. However, the existing road structure is not appropriate. It should be adapted to this target, by the investment in a network of roads that would emphasize the Secondary Centers and the Regional Centers as meeting points.

The average data on the amenities such as water supply, energy supply, telephones, and banks show higher levels in the centers than in the surrounding municipalities as could be expected. A relative abundance of such amenities in the centers increases the attractiveness of the centers and stimulates economic development. However, it should be noted that the level of supply of those amenities is still lower in the Secondary and Regional Centers than in Fortaleza.

The last two columns of Table 8 show the crucial role played by the Sao Jose Project for the solution of the development problem of the more isolated regions. The stimulation of stronger Secondary and Regional Centers would certainly help in the development of their regions and to some extent also of the more isolated municipalities (as said above, all municipalities are at an accessible distance from the main urban centers). However, there is no doubt that the more isolated places would benefit less than others from such a spatial reorganization, and therefore special focused treatment is needed.

Table 8. Supporting Infrastructures.

Region	Distance to Closest SC or RMF	Distance to Fortaleza	Road Density	% with Water Supply	% with Energy Supply	Residential Energy p/c 1995–1999	Telephones per 100 Habitants 1997	Banks per Thousand Habitants 1997	S.J.: Intensity Index for Supported Families	S.J.: R$ p/c
Total	90	270	0.50	33	61	0.22	2.51	0.030	1.0	14
RMF total: 13 mun.	26	26	0.64	28	82	0.37	4.57	0.035	0.0	1
Center: 1 mun.	0	0	0.98	97	96	0.44	21.00	0.075	0.0	0
Region: 12 mun.	28	28	0.61	21	80	0.21	3.20	0.031	0.2	2
SC total: 46 mun.	41	345	0.52	39	65	0.16	2.82	0.032	1.3	17
Centers: 7 mun.	8	368	0.52	66	83	0.22	6.73	0.057	0.7	9
Regions: 39 mun.	46	341	0.52	35	61	0.10	2.12	0.027	1.8	25
RC total: 79 mun.	107	256	0.53	34	58	0.11	2.38	0.034	1.6	25
Centers: 14 mun.	126	269	0.40	50	69	0.14	3.84	0.072	1.4	27
Regions: 65 mun.	102	252	0.54	31	56	0.09	2.12	0.027	1.7	24
Others total: 46 mun.	126	290	0.38	28	56	0.10	1.86	0.019	2.4	32
Secondary centers										
Sobral total	44	260	0.45	40	66	0.16	2.29	0.017	1.0	13
Sobral	0	230	0.22	81	99	0.24	6.31	0.043	0.2	4
Sobral region: 16 mun.	46	262	0.47	37	64	0.10	2.04	0.016	1.6	19
Limoeiro-Russas total	34	200	0.36	41	65	0.15	3.17	0.038	1.9	24
Limoeiro do Norte	0	198	0.26	41	71	0.18	7.90	0.066	2.0	18
Russas	38	160	0.37	47	71	0.17	4.68	0.057	2.0	23
Region: 6 mun.	39	207	0.37	40	63	0.13	2.13	0.030	1.8	27
Crajubar total	38	532	0.91	40	53	0.18	2.98	0.039	0.7	11
Crato	11	527	0.27	77	36	0.23	7.30	0.062	0.8	11
Juazeiro do Norte	0	538	1.35	99	100	0.24	7.20	0.042	0.1	0
Barbalha	10	538	0.60	50	73	0.15	3.43	0.068	0.4	7
Region: 8 mun.	50	530	0.98	26	54	0.08	1.86	0.033	1.6	26
Iguatu total	44	403	0.34	38	64	0.14	3.28	0.043	2.0	27
Iguatu	0	386	0.58	69	85	0.22	10.26	0.063	1.4	20
Region: 9 mun.	49	405	0.31	34	62	0.11	2.50	0.040	2.2	29

The Sao Jose Project plays exactly this role, by offering infrastructure support mostly to the more isolated places. The indicator, which was used to measure that effect is the "intensity index" calculated in each municipality as its share of families benefiting from the Sao Jose support of total Ceara families that receive this support, divided by the share of the municipality in the whole population of Ceara. An index of 1 (as in the total) means that the municipality receives support in the same proportion as its share of the population. Whereas an index of more than 1 means that the municipality receives more support than its share in the population. The index is actually about 0 in the RMF, very low at the Secondary Centers themselves (excluding Limoeiro do Norte and Russas, which show a high index), and grows in their regions. It is higher in the regions of the Regional Centers and reaches a maximum at the isolated "other" regions, with an average value of 2.4: the share of families that benefit from the Sao Jose Project in those municipalities is 2.4 times greater than their share in the population. The allocations per capita of population in the municipalities, as shown in the last column of Table 8, reinforce this conclusion. We conclude that this is an important instrument for the achievement of a better spatial balance in the economic development of the interior and of a diminution of inequalities.

Our conclusion for this section is therefore:

1. The Secondary and Regional Centers actually show signs of their appropriateness to play the role of main urban centers.
2. There is still a need to reinforce the necessary infrastructures of water, energy, communication, etc., and especially the necessary road network that would establish their centrality in their regions.
3. The more isolated municipalities may benefit less than others from such a process and require a focused attention. The Sao Jose Project plays this role with much success and should therefore be reinforced.

8. SOCIAL INDICATORS

A positive trend regarding the potential for the diminution of gaps between the various groups of regions is demonstrated in Table 9.

The literacy rate is lower in the Secondary and Regional Centers than in the RMF, and lower in the regions than in the centers themselves. However, on a whole, the rate of literacy is on average equal in all groups of regions outside the bigger urban centers, independent of the location of the municipalities: the average literacy rate is not lower in the group of isolated municipalities than

Table 9. Social Indicators (per Thousand Population).

Region	Literacy Rate of Population 15+, 1995	Schooling Rate	Doctors IDM 99	Beds 1999	Infant Mortality 1999	Health Units, 1999	Libraries, Theaters, Museums 1999
Total	51	95%	1.21	2.3	38	0.33	0.029
RMF total: 13 mun.	64	90%	1.46	2.4	27	0.14	0.015
Center: 1 mun.	83	87%	2.63	2.9	20	0.11	0.015
Region: 12 mun.	62	98%	1.37	1.2	28	0.24	0.014
SC total: 46 mun.	51	95%	1.28	3.0	43	0.42	0.046
Centers: 7 mun.	63	95%	2.43	4.5	36	0.42	0.037
Regions: 39 mun.	49	96%	1.08	1.6	44	0.43	0.053
RC total: 79 mun.	49	100%	1.22	1.9	35	0.47	0.036
Centers: 14 mun.	53	101%	1.40	2.3	32	0.44	0.030
Regions: 65 mun.	49	100%	1.22	1.7	35	0.49	0.040
Others total: 46 mun.	49	99%	1.06	1.5	41	0.44	0.031
Secondary centers							
Sobral total	49	93%	0.77	2.4	46	0.43	0.043
Sobral	61	98%	2.29	4.3	41	0.42	0.013
Sobral region: 16 mun.	48	91%	0.68	1.1	46	0.43	0.063
Limoeiro-Russas total	57	97%	1.40	2.2	38	0.31	0.048
Limoeiro do Norte	66	96%	1.75	3.9	38	0.14	0.061
Russas	63	95%	1.45	2.1	42	0.42	0.035
Region: 6 mun.	54	98%	1.33	1.7	38	0.32	0.049
Crajubar total	52	94%	2.05	4.4	44	0.44	0.053
Crato	67	99%	3.55	10.5	34	0.67	0.077
Juazeiro do Norte	64	91%	1.51	2.7	40	0.26	0.024
Barbalha	64	87%	4.18	6.0	34	0.74	0.085
Region: 8 mun.	47	98%	1.67	2.1	47	0.44	0.067
Iguatu total	49	98%	1.21	2.0	40	0.47	0.036
Iguatu	58	100%	2.27	2.6	22	0.45	0.023
Region: 9 mun.	48	98%	1.09	1.8	42	0.48	0.040

in the groups of municipalities around the Secondary and the Regional Centers. Still, those rates are still too low and the efforts to increase it in all municipalities, including the major urban centers, should be continued.

According to the data on the schooling rates of the population of ages 7–14, these efforts are actually being made. Those rates reach about 100% in many municipalities; they are not less, on average, in all types of municipalities than those of the RMF (they are even higher). This variable indicates the actual action taken in the present to increase literacy and this will certainly show in higher literacy rates of the adult population in the future.

A similar picture appears with the data about health indicators and about the cultural indicator. The number of health units and the number of libraries, theaters, and museums per 1,000 populations are not lower in the interior than in the RMF, and it is more or less equal on average in all groups of municipalities in the interior. The number of doctors and the number of hospital beds per inhabitant is higher in the more central urban places, but this is a result of the natural concentration of central health services in bigger cities.

Concluding this section, we find a serious effort for the provision of social services in the fields of education and health as seen before in the fields of water and energy supply, on a more or less equal basis in all groups of municipalities. Still, equality has not been achieved and the efforts that were made in the last years should continue.

9. ELABORATION OF REGIONAL DEVELOPMENT PLANS

Detailed plans for regional development of four of these centers have been effected and published by planning firms following given directives: identification of the main economic basis, strengthening of the urban center with infrastructures and appropriate services, building of a regional network, services to the rural hinterland, housing and social services, and educational networks, etc. The plans have been elaborated in close cooperation with the Regional Councils or other bodies of regional social participation. The plans are used as an important anchor for the decisions made about the allocation of budgets at the state level.

The Regional Development Plans were elaborated on the basis of given strategic guidelines for the social and economic development of the regions:

- Outline the future of the regions in terms of the potentials and weaknesses that characterize such regions defining opportunities that bring about changes.

- Stimulate the development of a culture of self-management and implementation of an integrated process of regional planning.
- Design the patterns of collaboration between towns, institutions, and agents that act in the development of the region stimulating the participation and communication for a convergence of common interests.
- Indicate strategic options and structure-building projects to stimulate economic dynamism and promote social inclusion, compatible with its role as inducer of development in the interior of the state.
- Propose infrastructures of a regional character that permit the integration of the physical space, facilitate accessibility between urban nuclei and the regional public services, and serve as support to the consolidation of the main economic activities.

The Regional Development Plans included four main components: regional characterization, strategic plan, proposal for structuring the regional space, and implementation strategy.

The objective of the regional characterization component is the understanding of the regional space and its insertion in the state context, using databases at the municipal level.

The strategic planning component covers the following aspects:

- integrated vision of the region's advantages and potentials;
- identification of the obstacles and threats to be addressed in order to boost development opportunities;
- survey of the hierarchy and functions of the urban nuclei;
- elaboration of prospective scenarios for the region with demographic, socio-economic, and environmental dimensions;
- measures required to strengthen the regional economy, involving the business community and the local entrepreneurship; and
- elaboration of a methodology for the participation of the population in the elaboration and implementation of the Plan.

The regional space structuring component portrays the territorial ordering, indicating the infrastructure necessary for the implementation of the strategic plan, macro-zoning for the implementation of the activities, as well as a proposal for strengthening the regional urban network.

The implementation strategy relates to guidelines for the initiation of the development plan. The implementation strategy also includes the definition of structure-building projects within a hierarchy of priorities, a systematization of monitoring and feedback of the Plan, and a model for the management of the region.

REFERENCES

Banco do Nordeste do Brasil. (1978). Industrializacao Rural no Nordeste do Brasil, BNB, Fortaleza, Brazil.

Bar-El, R. (1990). Rural industrialization in Northeast Brazil: The importance of local towns. In: M. Mtewa (Ed.), *International development and alternative futures: The coming challenges* (pp. 323–336). New Delhi: Allied Publishers Limited.

Bar-El, R., & Parr, J. (2003). From metropolis to metropolis-based region: The case of Tel-Aviv. *Urban Studies*, *40*(1), 113–125.

Dickinson, R. E. (1947). *City, region and regionalism*. London: Routledge and Kegan Paul.

Governo do Estado do Ceara. (2004). Indice de Desenvolvimento Municipal, Ceara 2002, IPECE, Fortaleza, Brazil.

McKenzie, R. D. (1933). *The metropolitan community*. New York: McGraw Hill.

Parr, J. B. (1999). The metropolitan area in its wider setting. In: A. A. Summers, P. C. Cheshire, & L. Senn (Eds), *Urban change in the United States and Western Europe, comparative analysis and policy* (2nd ed., pp. 215–242). Washington: The Urban Institute Press.

Rondinelli, D. A. (1983). *Secondary cities in developing countries: Policies for diffusing urbanization*. Beverly Hills: Sage Publications.

Rondinelli, D. A., & Ruddle, K. (1978). *Urbanization and rural development: A spatial policy for equitable growth*. New York: Praeger Publishers.

Schmitt, B., & Henry, M. S. (2000). Size and growth of urban centers in French Labor market areas: Consequences for rural population and employment. *Regional Science and Urban Economics*, *30*, 1–21.

CHAPTER 7

SPATIAL ORGANIZATION

In order to respond to the needs for spatial restructuring and adaptation for a more equalitarian process of economic development, three major spatial organization measures were analyzed and later implemented by the Government, as follows:

1. A NEW SECRETARIAT FOR LOCAL AND REGIONAL DEVELOPMENT

The implementation of a new model for development with a focus on regional growth requires adaptation of the government administration to the new needs. A vital instrument for such an adaptation is the establishment of a new Secretariat in the government of Ceara, the Secretariat for Local and Regional Development (SDLR). Such a Secretariat was established by the newly elected government in 2003.

Such a Secretariat is expected to focus on the following main objectives:

- the reduction of poverty and of inter-regional inequalities;
- the social and economic growth of the Interior of Ceara; and
- the increase of social participation in the process of development.

Two main roles are assigned to the SDLR:

1. The role of facilitator: as such, it promotes the building of social capital by integrating social regional forces, identifying regional needs, and stimulating action for regional development by appropriate secretariats in line with those needs.
2. The role of developer: actions as a developer should be taken only in areas where there is no direct responsibility by an existing Secretariat.

In operational terms, the actions to be taken by SDLR can be defined primarily as:

- Elaboration of a global regional vision and of a regional master plan. Such a regional master plan should consider the whole space of Ceara, and integrate the approach of secondary and tertiary cities into an organizational rebuilding of government services on a regional basis.
- Support for rural and agricultural development by means of support to programs of technology upgrade and business orientation.
- Support for the development of non-agricultural activities in the rural area and in towns in the Interior, through the program of Consultoria Empresarial.
- Restructuring of regional development, through the Regional Development Plans.
- Support for the development of human capital.
- Building of social regional capital through the establishment of Regional Councils.

The instruments that facilitate the implementation of such actions and the achievement of the main objectives are:

- SDLR should concentrate on regional and local development in the Interior and not deal with the Metropolitan region. In the case where responsibility for the Metropolitan area stays with the SDLR, a separate unit should be allocated for that, so that the priority of the Interior is not affected.
- Regional Development Plans: a strong emphasis should be put on the continuous follow-up by the SDLR professionals to make sure, before anything else, that the planning process is actually following the main guidelines as elaborated in view of the needs for growth with equity.
- The promotion of policy measures with higher priority for regional development in the Interior can be achieved by the creation of a matching procedure by which the SDLR would participate in the financing of such measures by a certain percentage, which can move between 5 and 30%, depending on the priority attributed to each project and the impact of the participation on decision-making. This would be the basis for the coordination and cooperation between the SDLR and other secretariats.
- An additional instrument that can be used by the SDLR in order to achieve the target of increased priorities for regional development in the Interior is the allocation by the Government through the Secretariat of Planning of a part of the budgets of some secretariats (for example 20%)

for the reinforcement of interior regions. The use of this part of the budget by each secretariat would require the endorsement of the SDLR, and would be subject to follow-up evaluation.

- A separate budget should be allocated to SDLR for actions taken as a developer; such budget would be used for actions suggested by the Regional Councils and authorized by the Secretariat, direct investments by the SDLR, etc.

2. REGIONAL ECONOMIC DEVELOPMENT UNITS, OR REGIONAL OFFICES

The ability of peripheral regions to compete with economic activities at the state level is hindered mostly by the disadvantages that characterize many of them, which can be explained mainly by the lack of agglomeration or scale economies. Concrete examples are the small scale of markets, the limited access to specialized production factors and the lack of urbanization.

The general concept behind the regional economic development units is that the competitive ability of the peripheral regions in the interior can be improved by trying to reduce the constraints of the lack of agglomeration or scale economies, using a regional approach. In other words, the focused support to individual enterprises or municipalities may not be sufficient for the achievement of a competitive ability, and a significant element is to be added: the consolidation of the region as a whole. This means reinforcement of the links between the various economic activities, cooperation between various economic forces that can increase the benefits of each of them, improvement of regional conditions such as infrastructures or educational facilities that can increase the economic efficiency of most individual economic activities, cooperation between the various economic and social leaders in the community to achieve common regional goals, and coordination between the various public institutions at the national and local levels that act within the region. Such efforts would lead to the creation of reinforcement of the regional "social capital," considered today by most development specialists as a crucial element for the development of peripheral regions.

The establishment of regional economic development units seeks to empower the local and regional development forces and leaders. These regional units or regional offices are empowered to coordinate – at the local and regional level – the development efforts initiated by the local and central government or by the local population, and implement them in close contact with the local population. They coordinate the work of local and regional authorities currently operating in the area, integrating them with the state development institutions.

Nine regional development units have already been installed and are fully operational. Each unit covers a number of municipalities in a region, is operated by a manager at the regional office established for this purpose by the SDLR, under the guidance of a Regional Advisory Council.

This Regional Advisory Council consists of representatives of the local society (religious, educational, etc.), the local business community, the local politicians (mayors of all municipalities represented), and regional representatives of government offices. Such a regional council is expected to be a popular body that represents the various components of society and of government in the region. The council appoints "working groups" for specific purposes (such as the development of regional tourism, the organization of a regional exposition) that operate under the guidelines of the council and with the support of the manager of the regional office.

Beyond the nine regional offices that have already been established, there are plans to establish such offices in each of the secondary and tertiary regions. Most of the action is oriented toward the attraction of entrepreneurs, stimulation of the creation of appropriate economic conditions in the region for the development of economic activities: fostering economic projects (such as infrastructure) based on regionally defined criteria.

The effects of such regional units (or offices) as identified with experience until now are:

- Empowerment of regional forces through the development of a "regional social capital," acting through the regional councils, with the representation of local and regional, social, economic, political leaders in full coordination with government representatives.
- Increased synergy between all regional elements of economic growth, increasing productivity, and competitiveness.
- Increased externalities, by solving regional (not just local) bottlenecks and by "marketing" the region as a whole.
- Increased coherence between local, regional, and state economic development.

In sum, the regional offices together with their regional councils may in the long-term be a leading institutional power for economic growth, with a broad vision of local, regional, and state elements, all represented in their administration. They should be considered as the Government instrument for the achievement of a process of local regional participation in the growth process on one hand, and for the coordination of actions of other government agencies on the other hand.

3. THE TECHNOLOGICAL IMPROVEMENT PROGRAM

An additional program that is intended to improve productivity and the multiplier effect was launched in three pilot regions. The main objectives of this program are:

- To provide technological guidance individually or in groups with common interest.
- To organize sectoral groups with the aim of meeting technological needs and developing innovative programs.
- To support the technological demands of the firms served by the monitoring program.
- To facilitate access to the financing sources in order to meet the demands of the groups or the firms for the technological solution indicated.
- To identify new production paradigms for the region based on technological knowledge.
- To identify and reveal the technological investment opportunities in the region.
- To identify the technological capacity needs of the productive agents in the region and to propose service solutions.
- To stimulate collaboration between the firms and the research institutions.
- To promote mobilization, propagation, and sensitizing events.

An "Innovation Agent" was appointed for each region. An example of some of the activities carried out by the Regional Innovation Agent in the Cariri region may serve to illustrate the nature of his task. He identified 25 ceramics entrepreneurs that needed technological assistance; succeeded in organizing six of them into a group, and assisted them in determining their deficiencies and how these deficiencies could be solved; he assisted the group in the preparation of a technological training agreement with CENTEC in the development of new products, and in caring for the environment; he organized a meeting with civil construction companies of the region to discuss the introduction of new ceramics products; he organized a special course on partnership between researchers and industry looking for ways to transfer innovation from the research institutions to commercial use.

PART IV
SOLVING LOCAL FAILURES – MICRO-REGIONAL POLICY

CHAPTER 8

INCREASING FACTOR PRODUCTIVITY IN THE RURAL AREA

The gaps in labor productivity between the rural and urban sector (or between Ceara and other states of Brazil) are alarming both in terms of their contribution to poverty and their significance for competitive ability. In our evaluations above, we evaluated the potential contribution of increased productivity at a level of 3–4% a year.

Lower labor productivity in the rural area is a result of low-levels of achievement of the three main production factors: labor force (low-levels of human capital), capital (low access to finance), and infrastructures (low or inappropriate infrastructures for the changing economy). Increasing the efficiency of these factors is actually considered an improvement of the so-called "total factor productivity" (TFP). Increasing TFP is mainly the responsibility of public policy, in terms of the supply of external conditions that lead to increased production. Those conditions are generally identified as the provision of education services, professional training, physical infrastructures, technology development, and appropriate conditions of public management and macroeconomic structures. An increase in TFP would lead to greater marginal productivity of labor and capital in the business sector, thereby increasing salaries and the return to private investment capital. In practical terms, the measures taken by the state government in order to increase agricultural productivity, increase education-levels, and build physical infrastructures are positive examples in that direction. However, the persistence of quite low average levels of productivity requires the consideration of additional measures for the improvement of productivity. A few policy strategies are examined here, in terms of the three above-mentioned production factors.

1. HUMAN CAPITAL

1.1. A General Picture

Education is probably the most important instrument for the improvement of human capital. It leads to greater productivity and therefore to higher levels of income and the diminution of poverty, an increase in employment flexibility, a greater accessibility to wider employment opportunities, the stimulation of various services and consumer products, and more. The influence of education is proven worldwide. A World Bank study (unpublished) finds that the return from education in Northeast is high, especially in the rural area. It also shows that higher levels of education increase the probability of non-farm employment. The study of the Banco do Nordeste do Brazil (1978) on rural industrialization of the Northeast found, on the basis of an econometric model, that education is a major stimulant of urban-oriented industrialization in the interior. A specific study of small agro-industrial firms in Ceara by Pinto (1994) also concludes that education and professional training is one of the most important necessities of such rural activities.

The state policy has for many decades been oriented to heavy investments in education; such a policy has proved effective and led to a continuous increase in the level of education of the population. However, this increase in the level of education is not yet sufficient and gaps between the rural and urban population are still high, as can be seen in Table 1.

As can be seen in Table 1, there has been a continuous decrease of the share of population with no schooling (or less than a year), from 71% in 1960 to 29% in 1997. In this same period, the share of population with higher levels of education kept increasing. For example, the share of population with 11 years or more of schooling increased from <1% to more than 10%.

The increasing share of population with higher levels of education and the decreasing share of population with low-levels of education is clear in both the urban and rural sectors. However, this trend of improving education is much more marked in the urban sector, leading to increasing gaps between the urban and rural sectors. This is clearly shown by the rural/urban ratio in the table. A ratio of 1 indicates a similarity between the two sectors. The findings in Table 1 do not show any convergence trend toward the value of 1. On the contrary, the rural/urban ratio of the percent of the population with the lowest levels of education (<1 year) is greater than 1 and, most important, it constantly increased during the entire 37-year

Table 1. Distribution of Population 5 Years Old and Over by Years of Schooling (%).

	Total	less than 1	1 to 3	4 to 7	8 to 10	11 to 14	15 or more	Unknown
Distribution (%)								
1960	**100.0**	**71.4**	**20.4**	**6.1**	**1.2**	**0.7**	**0.2**	**0.0**
Urban	100.0	53.0	26.3	15.0	3.3	1.9	0.6	0.0
Rural	100.0	80.9	17.4	1.5	0.1	0.0	0.0	0.0
1970	**100.0**	**67.4**	**19.9**	**8.5**	**2.1**	**1.8**	**0.4**	**0.0**
Urban	100.0	48.3	24.8	17.2	4.7	4.1	0.9	0.0
Rural	100.0	81.0	16.3	2.3	0.2	0.1	0.0	0.0
1980	**100.0**	**55.8**	**21.7**	**14.6**	**4.0**	**3.2**	**0.7**	**0.1**
Urban	100.0	39.4	24.1	22.4	6.9	5.8	1.3	0.1
Rural	100.0	75.0	18.9	5.5	0.5	0.2	0.0	0.0
1991	**100.0**	**42.8**	**23.6**	**19.6**	**6.3**	**6.2**	**1.6**	**0.0**
Urban	100.0	32.5	23.3	24.0	8.8	9.0	2.3	0.0
Rural	100.0	62.6	24.1	11.0	1.6	0.6	0.0	0.0
1997[a]	**100.0**	**28.7**	**26.1**	**25.6**	**8.5**	**8.6**	**2.2**	**0.2**
Urban	100.0	20.3	22.6	30.1	11.4	12.1	3.3	0.2
Rural	100.0	46.5	33.6	16.0	2.4	1.1	0.1	0.3
Rural/urban ratio[b]								
1960	1.00	1.53	0.66	0.10	0.03	0.02	0.02	0.47
1970	1.00	1.68	0.66	0.13	0.05	0.03	0.01	0.39
1980	1.00	1.90	0.78	0.25	0.07	0.03	0.02	0.20
1991	1.00	1.93	1.03	0.46	0.18	0.07	0.02	0.36
1997	1.00	2.30	1.49	0.53	0.21	0.09	0.02	1.22

Source: Elaboration of data from Demographic Census (IBGE, various years, a) and PNAD (IBGE, various years, b).

[a]Data for 1997 refer to the population aged 10 and over.

[b]Equal to the ratio of the % of population at each schooling years category in the rural area divided by the % of population at the same schooling years category in the urban area.

period, from 1.53 in 1960 to 2.30 in 1997. Such a growing gap, despite the fact of a global increase in education-levels, continuously weakens the ability of the rural sector to be competitive with urban sector, and leads to growing poverty gaps and lower development abilities. We should also indicate that, on the other hand, the share of persons with relatively high-levels of education (11 years or more) has grown in the rural area at a greater rate than in urban area. However, this phenomenon has a negative side effect: an increase of the relative gap within the rural sector. We now find in the rural sector a growing relative number of persons with no education, as well as a growing relative number of persons with quite high-education-levels and occupation expectations.

In sum, it seems that the enormous efforts invested in education have led to a drastic improvement, but at the same time to a growing gap between the rural and urban sectors. The share of the investments in the rural area should grow at a much faster rate than urban area, in order to enable a diminution of gaps, or even prevent the gaps from growing. The percentage of persons with only 3 years or fewer of education has dropped drastically, but it still stands at 80% in the rural area.

The data for 1999 show a continuation of the trend of increasing education. The share of non-educated persons (<1 year of schooling) has decreased to 24% in total. In Table 2, comparing Ceara with the Northeast and other regions in 1999, we find that the gaps are still high: the share of non-educated population in Ceara and the Northeast is about twice that of Brazil as a whole, and almost three times that the Southeast. However, it is important to observe a diminution of the rural/urban gap in the last several years: 2.04 in 1999, compared with 2.30 in 1997. Moreover, the rural/urban gap is lower in Ceara than both Brazil as a whole and the Southeast. The same picture appears with the analysis of data on illiteracy: it is much higher in Ceara than Brazil or the Southeast, but the rural/urban gap is lower.

Concluding this issue, we can state that the education gap between Ceara and other regions in Brazil is still very large, and therefore the lack of improvement in education-levels is still the case in the state as a whole, mainly in the rural area, in spite of all the efforts that have already been invested. The rural–urban gaps are lower in Ceara than other regions in Brazil, but they have been increasing for many years, and the recent trend of

Table 2. Illiteracy and Education in 1999 by Region.

	CE	NE	SE	BR
% Illiteracy out of population of 5+ years				
Total	30%	29%	10%	16%
Urban	23%	21%	8%	12%
Rural	44%	42%	20%	30%
Rural/urban ratio	1.90	1.97	2.41	2.54
% with less than 1 year of schooling, out of population 10+ years of age				
Total	24%	24%	9%	13%
Urban	18%	18%	7%	10%
Rural	37%	37%	18%	26%
Rural/urban ratio	2.04	2.06	2.39	2.59

Source: Elaboration of PNAD data for 1999 for each region, Tables 3.1 and 3.2.

decrease should be reinforced by investing greater shares of resources in the rural area.

In addition to the regular educational programs, a few new types of programs should be considered in an effort to achieve the goals of diminution of gaps in education and increasing human capital. A few ideas are presented here; some are already in the process of consideration by the state government.

1.2. Educational Reinforcement for Youngsters

These are programs for young pupils and students, with a focus on the medium- and long-term. The programs are designed to provide a response to the disadvantages faced by small rural localities because of the economies of scale that are inherent in educational investments. As part of this approach, a special program is intended for outstanding students, with the goal of fostering an atmosphere in which the rural sector enjoys equal opportunities.

Objective: Provide youngsters with the tools to be prepared for a better employment future, in a rural or urban area.

Measures:

(1) Establish computer classrooms in local schools, and e-learning programs especially for the rural area students.
(2) Operate afternoon programs, either within the school or in after-school clubs (community centers) with computer classes.
(3) Establish a program by students helping younger students. This can be integrated into the academic framework of secondary schools, CENTEC, colleges, and universities. Perhaps the program could also be offered in an elementary school framework, whereby the older students work with younger students.
(4) "A computer for each student": a network for the distribution and maintenance of donated, second-hand computers to interested students. Tax benefits might be offered to large companies who donate computers.
(5) Establish at the regional universities (or CENTECs) afternoon, evening, and summer programs for science-oriented students from the rural area and local towns.
(6) Establish a parent–children (afternoon, evening, or summer) program for science-oriented adults and youths from the rural area and local towns.

(7) Establish a distance learning project for high schools in the interior.
(8) Teachers should undergo in-service training in the use of computers, and computer programs should be included in the curriculum.
(9) Establish in the local town a residential educational facility for excellent students from the rural area.

At the level of university education, the following measures are suggested for consideration:

(1) Establish a State Open University: Course of studies based on "study kits," correspondence, and occasional meetings. The Open University can be operated by one of the existing universities, or a consortium of universities.
(2) Support Regional Colleges: Concentrate on teaching, with less focus on academic research. Adapt fields of study to regional needs.
(3) Distance Learning Project for the Interior: It is recommended to establish a new educational organization of "Distance Learning" for the interior. It will be based on university courses in a fully written format, which are distributed to students' homes by mail coupled with weekly meetings with academic instructors to monitor the progress of the students. Virtual meetings, using videoconference facilities, can replace the weekly meetings. It is suggested that preparation of the written courses be under the responsibility of one of the universities in a secondary city and that video conference facilities be built in each of the secondary cities and regional towns. The broadcasting studios for transmitting of courses will be located at the university, which is responsible for the Distance Learning Project.

1.3. "Working and Learning" Programs: Education for the Adult Population

The following programs are intended to combine educational activities with employment activity. Two kinds of programs should be considered: one for the population engaged in rural area activities, and another for the population employed in industry.

1.3.1. "Working and Learning": Rural Area

Extensive investments are made in the rural sector in human capital as well as infrastructures, land, and business capital. However, a significant part of the workforce still has a low-level of education that impairs their ability to exploit these means of production. For example, farmers with poor (if any) literacy skills, find it difficult to adopt new technologies, examine the feasibility of new crops, etc. This leads to lower levels of productivity and risk-taking. Farmers overestimate the level of risk inherent in any change, whether in management or technologies, and it is difficult to generate change. This also claims a price in terms of lower returns on investments in production schemes sponsored by the state.

The proposed program is intended for the working population, with the objective of improving the productivity of the labor force in short-term. Improving the level of education will increase the productivity of this population, stimulate the adoption of new technologies, and help them in the future to find non-agricultural employment outside the rural area.

It is proposed that basic study programs, including reading and writing, be integrated into the existing rural support programs, and include the development of an appropriate framework of incentives. Several levels of basic studies may be defined: Level 1: basic reading and writing; Level 2: arithmetic and improving reading and writing; Level 3: basic commercial concepts. Studies may take place in groups (even of 4–6 persons), close to the participants' place of residence. A basic study kit can be prepared and distributed to participants. Objective criteria can be defined for examining the level of achievements, as well as criteria for the selection of bodies authorized to provide training. Existing programs may be adapted for this purpose.

The objective of such programs is to increase the ability of more advanced production technologies to penetrate the rural sector and improve productivity in rural businesses. The measures to be taken are:

(1) Encourage participants of the existing support programs (PRONAF, SAO JOSE, Agrarian Reform) to participate in adult training programs.
(2) Or: Set the adult training program as a condition for entering various existing support programs (PRONAF, Sao Jose, Agrarian Reform).
(3) Establish a prize system for the achievement of good results in the education program (such as increased grants).
(4) Allocate special additional educational funds for *municipios* with high-achievement levels.
(5) Encourage competition between *municipios* at the regional- and/or national-levels.
(6) Establish criteria and framework for quality control and achievements. The criterion for success will be partly determined in relative terms, i.e., relative to conditions in the region and/or according to the level of progress.

1.3.2. "Working and Learning": Human Capital for Industry

In this case, the combination of working and learning is made at the place of work in industry, and the industrial owner is put in charge. The idea here is to stimulate working places to provide wider education and training for their workers, in order to improve the educational level and productivity in the longer range. The measures to be considered in order to achieve this goal can be the following:

(1) Subsidies for training workers in industry, on the condition that at least half of the training is carried out within educational institutions.
(2) Subsidy of 40% of salary during the training period and 80% of training costs.
(3) Training is for at least 20 h, and no more than 1 year.
(4) Thirty hours of expert consultancy for a firm taking part in a training program, 10 h fully subsidized and 20 h 75% subsidized.

1.4. Establishment of Institutional Frameworks for Human Capital Development

Establishment of a council for human capital development at the state-level, and local committees for human capital development at the regional-level is suggested.

1.4.1. Council for Human Capital Development

The role of this council would be to set priorities for educational programs and set long-term plans for their implementation. As a first step, a tender for the preparation of an Education Master Plan for the interior should be issued. The guidelines for such a Master Plan could be the following:

(1) Diminution of gaps in education achievements between the interior and RMF, and between the urban and rural area in the interior.
(2) Evaluation of the needs for vocational training.
(3) Reinforcing technology education
(4) Strengthening the link between educational institutions in the region and economic activity.
(5) Adaptation of educational and vocational training to the specific conditions and needs in each region.
(6) Special programs to improve the level of learning and teaching in the schools.
(7) Special programs for young people who have dropped out of school.

1.4.2. Local Committees for Human Capital Development

Such local (municipal or regional) committees for human capital development would act under the council. Their role would be to evaluate specific local needs and adapt the human capital development efforts to those needs. The members of these local committees may be from the educational sector, business sector, municipalities, local social institutions, and state. Main functions to be considered are:

(1) Suggest priorities for education and training programs.
(2) Establish principles for the application of existing and new programs.
(3) Initiate partnerships between the local educational institutions and business sector.
(4) Design contests and other incentives to achieve higher educational levels in local communities.

2. INFRASTRUCTURES

Public investment in infrastructures is one of the most important policy measures that stimulate economic activity, in both the agricultural and non-agricultural sectors. By infrastructure, we mean roads, airports, water supply, energy supply, sewage networks, industrial facilities, communication facilities, etc. Investment in infrastructure has a consumer perspective, through its contribution to the quality of life (such as appropriate water or electricity supply or communication networks), and also a producer perspective. The availability of better infrastructures is considered to be an increase in one of the production factors, and therefore increases the marginal productivity of the other production factors, e.g., capital and labor. This is expected to lead to a higher return in capital and labor, and consequently to a greater attraction of business capital investments and labor supply. The importance of public investments in infrastructures has a consensus among Ceara policy makers, and actually a high priority has been given to such investments in the rural area. This refers both to investments that are directly related to agricultural activity, such as dams and irrigation projects, as well as investments that are mostly related to non-farm activities. Infrastructure investments are part of many of the projects that are oriented toward the agricultural reforms, rural industrial development, and fight against poverty.

A detailed analysis of the investments in the various components of infrastructures in the rural area is much beyond the scope of this paper, and we prefer to focus on one specific policy aspect. It is what can be called "normative" decision-making for the priorities in public investments in infrastructures. There is a natural tendency to invest primarily in regions in the interior in which the greatest pressure is for improving infrastructures. This is of course natural and is expected to provide responses to the revealed needs of the population. This is also one of the components of the Sao Jose project, which considers the bottom-up demands for infrastructure investments and tries to meet those demands by using participatory practices. However, we should remember that there might be a "market failure" in the behavior of public investments in infrastructures. This failure results from the fact that infrastructures are not a free market commodity: those who benefit from it do not have to pay directly for its cost. Consequently, there may be cases where the revealed demand for infrastructures is lower than in other cases, but the long-term expected return is much greater. The government should, for example, give a lower priority to public investments in infrastructure in a region that expresses demand for the development of low-income non-farm employment linked to traditional low-income agriculture, and favor investments in a region where the long-term agricultural and non-agricultural potential is much greater, although there may be no expressed demand at the present. Investment in infrastructure may naturally be based on expressed needs, but it should mainly be of a planned nature, considering long-term needs, multiplier effects, and broad regional and state benefits. In short, we mean that infrastructure investment is an endogenous variable in development (responding to development needs), but it should be much more of an exogenous variable, inducing development.

The policy of treating infrastructure investment as exogenous has been implemented by the government of Ceara since 2002, through the establishment of government budget rules that allocate given shares of the budget by regions.

3. CAPITAL

One of the major problems that explain low-levels of productivity in the rural area is the low accessibility to finance. There are a few tracks for finance, but they do not always answer the needs of the local entrepreneurs, especially the needs for working capital. A few suggestions are made here for the alleviation of this problem, in already existing support programs.

3.1. PRONAF

PRONAF is a federal program that provides loans for entrepreneurs from the rural sector who meet various criteria. The criteria for eligibility, as well as the amount and conditions of the loan vary according to the type of entrepreneur, stage of the agrarian reform, income levels, and source of employment. Entrepreneurs are divided into four categories – A, B, C, and D. In most cases, loans are given at a single point in time; Category A loans are for 10 years; C for 5 years; and D for 8 years. For category B only, loans are given for 2 years, with the possibility of renewing the loan up to 3 times. Part of the loan converts to a grant for farmers who meet given conditions. It is suggested to:

- Make funds available for working capital.
- Make it possible to receive additional loans from the banking system before repaying the existing loans.

3.2. San Jose: Infrastructure

Each *municipio* prepares a municipal plan for rural development (PMDRM), which is approved by the CEDR. Each *municipio* provides 10% complementary funding, and takes responsibility for the ongoing maintenance of infrastructures. This approach offers numerous advantages – the development of social infrastructure, and decision-making on the local-level with the involvement and commitment of the local population.

The proposals below are intended to add the regional aspect to existing considerations, while maintaining the function and involvement of the local-level. The current situation is that decisions relating to the infrastructure program are made on the level of the individual *municipio*, rather than on the regional-level. The idea is to promote collaboration among several *municipios* in geographic proximity.

The importance of the regional dimension in the field of infrastructures relates to the fact that, in terms of the ramifications for potential economic development, physical contiguity of infrastructures is important. Regional activity offers advantages of increasing externalities in terms of size in investments and of the operation and maintenance of infrastructures. By way of example, the existence of a road in one locale that does not continue into the neighboring locale does not permit efficient use of the road. Similarly, inadequate maintenance in one locale may hamper development on the regional-level. The following proposals are intended to maintain the existing framework of the local-level since, as noted, we believe this to be the correct approach. However, the regional dimension must be added.

It is, therefore, recommended to consider the addition of finance for infrastructures at the regional-level to the existing track of finance for the development of infrastructures in each separate municipality. For that purpose an efficient measure may be the establishment of a regional forum representing the *municipios* of the region that would consider priorities between infrastructure regional projects, and be responsible for infrastructure maintenance.

3.3. Fund for Production Expansion

In order to facilitate the expansion of small businesses and their penetration into wider markets, the following measures are suggested to establish a fund with two tracks:

- *Track 1*: For financing market studies: evaluation of market potential, preparation of market surveys and marketing plans, cost of penetration into new markets, fairs, etc.
- *Track 2*: For the cost of the first stage of networking activity.

Consideration of the establishment of a venture capital fund, initially government-owned and privatized at a later stage, is also suggested.

REFERENCES

Banco do Nordeste do Brasil. (1978). *Industrializacao rural no Nordeste do Brasil*. Fortaleza, Brazil: BNB.

IBGE (Instituto Brasileiro de Geografia e Estatistica). (Various years, a). Censo Demografico do Brasil, Ministerio de Planejamento e Orcamento, Rio de Janeiro, Brazil.

IBGE (Instituto Brasileiro de Geografia e Estatistica). (Various years, b). Pesquisa Nacional por Amostra de Domicilios (PNAD), Ministerio de Planejamento e Orcamento, Rio de Janeiro, Brazil.

Pinto, F. J. (1994). *Diagnostico e perspectivas da micro e pequena agroindustria de fruto tropical no estado do Ceara*. M.A. thesis, Universidade Federal do Ceara, Fortaleza, Ceara, Brazil.

CHAPTER 9

RURAL NON-FARM EMPLOYMENT POLICY

The need for the development of non-farm activities in the interior of the state is strongly explained by a few additive factors as analyzed below:

1. The excess labor force in rural area is as a result of the inability of agriculture to provide sufficient employment to the growing population.
2. The evaluation that migration to the metropolitan region of Fortaleza is unable to provide a solution for all the excess labor force.
3. The inevitable process of urbanization in the interior of the state and consequent need for the growth of economic activities in non-agricultural sectors.
4. The additional excess labor force that will result from the imperative need for the increase of productivity in the agricultural sector, leading to a decreasing demand for workers, which cannot be met by the increase in agricultural activity.

The consequence is therefore that the solution for employment in the rural area (in the broad sense of the interior of the state, including local towns) is significant investment in the creation of employment opportunities in non-farm activities. As calculated in the scenarios above, such jobs would be partly within the rural area itself, but the majority would be jobs in industry and services mainly in the local cities. Such policy measures are vital in order to facilitate migration from the rural area to local cities, enable the growth of rural productivity, and decrease unemployment and poverty in the cities.

Most of non-farm employment in the rural area (as in the urban area) is actually in the sector of services. Evaluations made by the Ferreira and Lanjouw (2001) study, based on original data of PNAD in 1996, show that in the rural Northeast, less than a third of non-farm employment is in industry, including mining and extraction, including construction as a major branch of activity (about a third of all industrial employment).

A comparison with the distribution of non-farm employment in rural Southeast shows a quite similar picture, with a slightly higher relative weight of industry (about a third of employment).

The types of industrial activity in the rural sector are generally classified as manufacturing of agricultural products, production of inputs to agriculture, and non-agricultural related products, for local consumption or exports of the region. The formal classification of industrial activities does not permit an appropriate analysis of data in this respect. Still, we can use some indicators to evaluate the potential of various types of non-farm activities, as follows:

1. AGRICULTURE-RELATED NON-FARM ACTIVITIES

A relatively high share of employment is in food processing (about 5% of total non-farm employment), indicative of the tendency for agricultural processing activities, both in the Northeast and Southeast. Most employment, however, is not related to the agricultural sector, for example, ceramics and wooden goods that represent mainly artisan production or textiles that may be related to cotton production. However, these are mostly justified by the existence of a low-cost labor force.

There is no doubt about the comparative advantage of non-farm activities that are related to agriculture, both in terms of the processing of agricultural production (such as food processing, textiles) and supply of inputs and services for agricultural activity. The policy of stimulation of such activities by providing solutions for constraining factors such as infrastructures, credit, and administrative and professional support, is certainly important and should be continued. However, the potential and benefits of policy support for such activities are quite limited. Here are some main reasons:

1. Many of such rural-related activities are naturally located there, such as construction and direct services to agriculture, and do not need any stimulation policy.
2. The potential for such activities is directly linked to growth of agricultural activity, which is limited. The scenario used here assumes a growth of agricultural production of 3% a year, which is quite ambitious, but still lower than the growth of the state economy as a whole. The natural decrease of agriculture in total product leads directly to a decrease of the potential of agriculture-related activities.

3. The comparative advantage of proximity to agricultural production constantly loses weight in location decision-making, because of the continuously decreasing relative weight of communication and transportation factors, and globalization. This may not be true for highly perishable agricultural products, but inputs to agriculture such as pesticides or agricultural instruments may easily be imported from more distant regions. Even the textile industry may be located further from the cotton production (or at least in some of its later processing stages), given competitive salaries and other conditions.

The conclusion is that although agriculture-related non-farm activities should receive high priority because of their inherent advantages and multiplier effect, most of the non-farm employment will still have to be in other sectors. Their share of non-farm employment is already bigger, and it is expected to grow more rapidly. In this case policy measures are much more crucial, since the rural area has to compete successfully with other regions. In the next section, we shall refer to the potential of activities related to local demand, and later to activities that compete in external markets.

2. LOCAL DEMAND-ORIENTED NON-FARM ACTIVITIES

Rural non-farm activity is defined as agro-industry, processing of local production of agricultural products, and supplying inputs to agricultural activity only at a preliminary stage of development. The process of regional development creates a growing demand for local consumers' demand for goods and services. At a second stage of regional development, local demand for goods and services provides a basis for the growth of additional non-farm activity. Beyond the basic demand for food and elementary services that characterize the lowest level of development, a growing demand for more advanced products and services may arise at a more advanced stage. Such a demand may provide employment opportunities in various economic fields. If the rural region is ready for the development of economic activities that can meet this potential demand, those can be a source of additional dynamic growth. Otherwise, some of this demand may be met by imports from other regions, thus increasing economic dependence and decreasing the potential for endogenous economic growth. The extent of such a demand and economic ability of the region to meet it should be evaluated for the various products and services as a function of different variables, such as the income elasticity of demand for each product or service, expected growth of population and income, level of tradability of each product or service (ability to purchase it from distant places), competitive advantage of the region, and production function of each product (mainly in terms of capital or labor intensity).

The relative weight of these types of non-farm employment may increase continuously in relation to the demand for agriculture-related employment. This results from the fact that the demand for consumer goods and services increases quite rapidly (as a function of growing population and income), while the demand for agriculture-related activities are constrained by the limits of agricultural growth. In fact, this growing demand is a main stimulator of urbanization at later stages.

Assuming a quite high-level of 5% annual economic growth, and using some rough evaluations of income elasticities of demand and production functions for local demand products, the expected growth of local demand for employment in order to meet the growing consumption is about 5–6%. This includes high relative growth rates in goods and services, with high-income elasticities of demand such as education, clothing, transport, personal services, recreation, and culture, and low relative growth rates in goods and services with low-income elasticities of demand, such as food or cigarettes. Those findings provide an interesting picture of the sectors in which the potential for employment growth is expected to be the highest. However, two important conclusions should be emphasized:

1. The total growth of demand for local goods and services can provide only a 5–6% growth of employment in the rural area, while the needed growth of non-farm employment in order to achieve the development goals was estimated at 18%. This means that local demand cannot be the main stimulator of non-farm employment growth, and its share of total non-farm employment is expected to decrease.
2. Most local goods and services are not necessarily provided by the local labor force. Growth of the local supply is highly dependent on the development of competitive advantages in the rural area; the growth of productivity as analyzed above is crucial for the growth of non-farm employment for local demand. Education, recreation (tourism), and personal services are fields in which the demand for labor is more locally oriented, and therefore their relative rapid growth may supply significant employment opportunities.

3. EXPORT-ORIENTED NON-FARM ACTIVITIES

The findings until now lead to the conclusion that the most important potential for non-farm employment is in export-oriented activities. By export, we mean all economic activity that is not directly related to local markets: it may be export to the metropolitan region of Fortaleza, other states in the Northeast or Brazil, or other countries. Both local agriculture and consumer demand are not sufficient for the supply of sufficient new employment in the rural area that would meet the needs of the suggested scenario and provide some solution to the rural poverty. A failure to do so will necessarily result in an increase in unemployment, a decrease of average income, an increase in poverty level, and the stimulation of increased migration from the interior to metropolitan region of Fortaleza.

The most important implication of such a conclusion is that the new rural economic activities will have to compete with the external economy, with no protection of local conditions or markets. This places important emphasis on policy measures, mentioned previously, connected with the increase of total factor productivity. This is coherent with the action suggested by the World Bank (2001) for the implementation of the strategy of fighting poverty by promoting opportunity. One of the measures suggested is expanding into international markets.

Given appropriate measures of public investment in physical and human infrastructures, the interior could offer opportunities for the attraction of a wide range of economic activities. In terms of manufacturing activities, the abundant and cheaper supply of land and labor force in the rural area may be attractive to industrial branches that do not heavily depend on concentrated markets and urban agglomeration economies. The globalization processes have greatly increased the flow of information, technology, knowledge, goods and services, and have enabled peripheral regions to compete in national and international markets (see da Rosa & Alves, 2000).

The feasibility of such a policy, on the basis of the trade behavior of Ceara in the last decade, is shown in Table 1.

Interstate interchange has grown in Ceara by 156% within a period of 8 years in the last decade, with an especially high growth of exports from Ceara to other states of Brazil, leading to a relatively decreasing share of deficit. At the same time, as has been shown above, the real growth of the GDP in Ceara was 31% (the whole of Brazil during the same time grew 23%). This clearly means that the share of exports of Ceara to other states out of its production rose rapidly and continuously. International interchange also increased rapidly, although data show that this mainly

Table 1. Ceara's Trade Interchange with Brazil and Foreign Countries: 1990–1998, in Millions of R$ at 1999 Prices.

	1990	1995	1998	% Growth 1990–1998
Interstate interchange	5,809	12,895	14,891	156
Export	2,105	5,093	6,202	195
Import	3,704	7,802	8,689	135
Balance	−1,599	−2,709	−2,487	56
International interchange	590	1,271	1,242	111
Export	404	448	459	14
Import	186	823	783	321
Balance	218	−375	−324	−249

Source: Internal data provided by the Ceara State Secretariat of Treasury. (Published with the permission of SEFAZ.)

represented increasing imports. However, the available data for the first 10 months of 1999 show a figure of rapidly growing exports (673 millions R$).

The conclusion is that, in order to keep up with the prevailing trends, rural industrial activities should integrate with the trend of globalization and penetrate into national and international markets. The state policy should therefore be oriented toward supporting efforts to increase the competitive ability of the rural industry in global markets. The main policy measures that should be considered are the following:

1. *Upgrading small-scale firms*: Stimulating small-scale industrial activities through the provision of basic infrastructures, facilities, and services is a beneficial policy. However, it is far from sufficient. The existence of a processing plant for fruits or milk, using basically traditional technologies, or concentrating in local markets, may be satisfactory in the short-term for the employment and basic income it supplies, but not as a long-term basic policy. Low-productivity levels of such plants prevent stimulation of long-term growth of both employment and income. Although support is already being offered today to those plants in terms of infrastructure, professional training, consulting in marketing, etc., but the results may be unsatisfactory in many cases. Improving technology, widening markets, increasing management efficiency – all these may provide external economies that would contribute to the economic growth of the region as a whole, and not just to the present local entrepreneurs. Therefore, measures should be considered for the stimulation of such external economies, such as the installation of

industrial "incubators," the conditioning of support upon the achievement of quality, technology and productivity standards, etc.

2. *Stimulating large-scale regional firms*: The availability of a larger supply of land at lower cost, supply of an abundant labor force, and decreasing cost of distance and communications, are advantages that may increase the competitive ability of firms in the rural area. Besides, the importance of small-scale activities that are closely linked to local production or markets, larger scale firms, on a regional basis, may be a more efficient instrument for integration into the national economy and creation of greater employment opportunities. The contribution of state intervention may be in the preparation of regional industrial parks, which can offer employment to a large radius of the rural labor force, and in the construction of roads or stimulation of transportation facilities.
3. *Supporting management and professional skills*: Various programs of support for industry, including professional training, consultancy in technology adaptation, marketing, and management, could improve productivity and competitive ability. Programs of this kind already exist, but they should be reinforced and given high priority. Special attention should be given to long-life learning programs, specific training courses provided to manufacturing firms, and monitoring programs that provide ongoing consultancy services to businesses. Finally, support in the identification of new markets and penetrating into new export markets could be provided.
4. *Upgrading of artisan production*: Artisan production is a quite significant source of income in Ceara, but its productivity could be increased by measures including better and more commercial management, with a stronger orientation toward export markets and greater production. Artisan products from many countries have reached the world market, and with some effort the interior regions of Ceara could exploit their comparative advantage and join this market.

4. RURAL TOURISM

Tourism is considered today as one of the most rapidly developing industries in the world and, for our purposes, it can be considered as an export-intensive activity (including exports to other states within Brazil). The prediction of the World Trade Organization (WTO) study on tourism in the year 2020 is an increase from about 668 million international tourists today to more than 1.5 billion. The total distances traveled by tourists are also expected to increase. The potential for increased activity in this economic branch is therefore quite significant. In fact, in Brazil as a whole, international tourism has continuously grown in the past several years, reaching an expected figure of about 4 million tourists in 2000.

The share of Ceara in international tourism is almost insignificant (55,000 in 1997), although it is strategically located for the tourists coming from Europe, the US, and Central America (a 3-h flight, shorter than to Rio de Janeiro or Sao Paulo from Europe or from the US). However, national tourism to Ceara is growing very rapidly, and has reached about 1 million persons a year, 40% of them coming from other states of the Northeast region, but also 30% from the Southeast (internal evaluations of the Banco do Nordeste do Brasil). Most of this tourism is now concentrated in Fortaleza and the coast, taking advantage of the consistently warm weather and beautiful seashore. In fact, Fortaleza has become one of the principal tourist cities in Brazil.

Rural tourism is a growing branch of economic activity all around the world, and there is a special new interest in the so-called pro-poor tourism (PPT) (Goodwin, 2000). Tourism can be used to diversify local economies, and it is generally less sensitive to agglomeration economies that manufacturing activity; it can be developed in marginal areas that can offer landscape, cultural, and wildlife values. The policies to enhance pro-poor tourism as suggested by Goodwin are, among others, putting poverty issues on the tourism agenda, enhancing a wide range of economic opportunities and their impact, adopting a multi-level approach (local, national, and international levels), and mainly incorporating pro-poor tourism approaches into mainstream tourism.

The idea of incorporating rural tourism into mainstream tourism is especially attractive with the prevailing conditions in Ceara. It would be difficult to attract considerable tourism to the interior alone, but the interior can consider using the potential of increasing numbers of tourists arriving to the metropolitan and coast region (see Steck, 1999, for the potential of tourism in small coastal communities). The trend of "integrated tourism," based on the provision of a package deal to tourists, could be very helpful for the development of tourism in the interior. There is a huge potential for tourists who visit Fortaleza mainly for seashore leisure, to be offered complementary tourism activities, enabling them to take advantage of the specific characteristics of the interior.

There is still a significant potential of growth of tourism both in Brazil and Ceara. The larger the mass of tourism to Fortaleza and the coast, the greater is the potential for attracting tourism to the interior. However, the existence of a potential market of tourists is a necessary but not a sufficient condition. An analysis of the touristic potential of the Sertao and Serras should be done, and the possibilities and conditions for the attraction of tourists who visit the coast should be investigated.

REFERENCES

da Rosa, A. L. T., & Alves, F. F. (2000). *Efeitos da Globalizacao Sobre a Economia Cearense*. Fortaleza, Ceara, Brazil: IPLANCE.

Ferreira, F. H. G., & Lanjouw, P. (2001). Rural nonfarm activities and poverty in the Brazilian Northeast. *World Development*, *29*(3), 509–528.

Goodwin, H. (2000). Pro-poor tourism: Opportunities for sustainable local development. *Development and Cooperation*, *5*, 12–14.

Steck, B. (1999). Potenciais de Paticipacao em Turismo para Comunidades de Pesca Artesanal nas Areas Litoraneas. Projetos Prorenda Rural dos Estados de Pernambuco e Ceara, Republica Federativa do Brasil.

World Bank. (2001). World development report 2000/2001: Attacking poverty, World Bank, Washington, DC.

CHAPTER 10

CONSULTANCY PROGRAM FOR SMALL- AND MEDIUM-SIZED ENTERPRISES

In collaboration with Dafna Schwartz

Within the global policy of demographic and economic restructuring of the interior, one of the programs that were implemented by the government of Ceara for the increase of productivity and competitiveness in the interior is the Consultancy Program for small- and medium-sized enterprises (SMEs).

The program brings in a consultant who initiates contact with the entrepreneur at the entrepreneur's premises and works with the entrepreneur to identify his main problems and provide solutions. When necessary the consultant directs the entrepreneur to other existing programs. The consultant also reports recommendations, including whether the entrepreneur should continue with consultancy services, and if so, in which specific areas and to what extent.

1. THE NEED FOR A SPECIAL CONSULTANCY PROGRAM

Peripheral areas generally have difficulties making the structural adjustments needed to accommodate national growth, and this in turn leads to growing unemployment rates, regional economic gaps, and continuous migration to metropolitan centers. SMEs located in rural areas or small towns are expected to play an important role in the process of economic development, absorbing excess labor force from agriculture, and leading the transition to non-farm employment (Leite, 1986). In practice, however, SMEs face substantial difficulties in their attempts to integrate into the national trends of economic growth. To a certain extent this can be attributed to the fact that management may possess inadequate skills and not have information at their disposal. In other cases, management may simply lack awareness of the importance of these fields.

Government support systems for SMEs may be effective for enterprises within a reasonable distance of urban or metropolitan areas, but they seem to lose most of their effectiveness for enterprises in remote areas. Such programs are mostly provided for groups of entrepreneurs within the urban sector, and may not be adapted to the needs and the characteristics of the peripheral rural sector. The outcome is that although there is potential need for the services among small- and medium-sized businesses based in remote areas, and although a wide range of support services for SMEs exists at the national and regional levels, these programs apparently face a market failure as they fail to achieve their objective in the remote areas, and consequently takeoff in those regions is considerably limited.

Our argument is that a discrepancy exists between the supply of consultancy support services by the government and demand for such services by the rural SMEs. The services that are offered by the support agencies do not always suit the conditions and needs specific to the given rural area, as they were designed primarily to service the needs of urban economic activity. Consequently, the needs of the rural SMEs are not met and the demand for such services may actually be a "hidden demand," not quite openly expressed as a result of the apparent lack of access to those services. Understanding where the actual supply and hidden demand intersect may provide important support for the ability of SMEs to resolve some of their business administration constraints, to increase their competitiveness, and to enable them to contribute to the integration of the peripheral area into national economic growth.

There is a discrepancy between supply and demand that can be explained by several related factors. The first is that supply is mostly focused on specific consultancy issues (such as marketing and administration), while rural SMEs face a diverse range of problems that emanate from the transition of a basically rural agricultural region to non-farm urban-like economic structures. The second is the inability of rural or remote SMEs to identify the main problems that hinder their efforts for economic success: they may ask for consultancy in a particular area when their main problem is really in a different area altogether. The third is that the geographic distance between the dispersed rural or remote SMEs and the consultancy services that are generally supplied in more central cities reduces accessibility and exposure to those services. The fourth is the lack of information as well as awareness the SMEs have of the potential differential contribution of consultancy services in various areas.

2. THEORETICAL BACKGROUND

A considerable number of recent studies have dealt with the importance of the contribution of SMEs in remote areas to regional development and with the difficulties faced by consultancy programs in trying to provide efficient support to the SMEs. The following short review is taken from Schwartz and Bar-El (2004).

Our starting point is that small businesses make a significant contribution to the local and regional economy, the community, and national economic growth. The importance of small businesses is in job and wealth creation and economic regeneration, mostly in the rural area in the peripheral regions. They contribute to creating new sources of income in regions where there is a reduction in agricultural sources of employment. Furthermore, they utilize unexploited means of production (infrastructure, labor force), encourage local entrepreneurship, and have a high local and regional multiplier. It is the small firms that tend to seek supplies, services, and capital from local businesses thus causing a positive spread effect on local businesses, while being less vulnerable to closures than branch establishments that have no loyalty to the local community and are influenced by external decisions (Henderson, Sutherland, & Turley, 2000; Winders, 2000).

However, despite their importance, small businesses encounter difficulties that hinder their development. A significant number of the problems are related to business aspects: management, business skill, and marketing deficiencies (Townroe & Mallalieu, 1990; Smallbone & Welter, 2001), obstacles in human resources (Huang & Brown, 1999), obstacles in the development of external linkages and network relations (Rothwell & Dodgson, 1991), difficulties linked to the institutional environment including bureaucracy (Ren, 1999; Bartlett & Bukvic, 2001), and the inability of existing financial institutions to cater to the needs of small business including the high cost of capital (Binks, 1979; Felsenstein & Schwartz, 1993; Deakins, 1999). The degree to which such firms are subject to difficulties, also depends to a large extent on their stage of development (Low & Abrahamson, 1997, make a distinction between emerging, growth, and mature industries) and upon the industrial sectors (North & Smallbone, 2000).

The assistance programs available in many states attempt to provide entrepreneurs with services to help them overcome these problems (Tendler & Amorim, 1996; Gibb, 1997; Chrisman, 1999; Lowe, Talbot, & Hannon, 2000; UNCTAD, 2000; Winders, 2000; Hjalmarsson & Johansson, 2003). It is, however, apparent that the entrepreneurs do not necessarily take advantage of the existing supply. In some cases, regardless of the availability and supply of services and the documented need for the said services, demand does not meet supply. As a result, the penetration rate of the assistance programs is low (Westhead & Storey, 1996; Curran & Blackburn, 2000; Patton, Marlow, & Hannon, 2000). This is especially crucial for the rural SMEs. Evidence from Latin America and Africa (Liedholm, 2002) shows that SMEs located in rural areas are less likely to survive during a given year than those located in the urban areas (by 25%).

The discrepancy between supply and demand is explained by the following factors:

- Distance to the location of service (Bennett, Bratton, & Robson, 2000), as time availability has been found to be a dominant factor in SMEs with regard to the acquisition of support services (Henderson et al., 2000): the services are frequently located in central locations at relatively long distances from the rural businesses.
- Lack of information regarding the assistance program (Patton et al., 2000) and of their potential contribution.
- Small businesses face multiple problems simultaneously, while the existing programs primarily focus on specific issues.
- The businesses also have difficulty diagnosing their main problem and may seek inappropriate expert assistance. One of the explanations for this is a lack of knowledge or motivation on the part of the business owner (as quoted in Huang & Brown, 1999; Clark, Berkeley, & Steuer, 2001).
- At times the problem is not a failure of identification, but rather the business owner's failure to focus on the main problems threatening the business either due to time and financial constraints (Devins, 1999) or because the business acts in response to events and not on the basis of rational long-term thinking (Gelderen, Frese, & Thurik, 2000).
- The solution of the business problems in many cases has to match the specific characteristic of the business and of the region, while the existing programs are often provided in groups and not on an individual basis.
- There are not enough consultants who are familiar with the characteristics of the periphery.
- Entrepreneurs may also be suspicious, lacking the trust and desire to reveal themselves to the establishment. SMEs seek advisory services through their network (Hjalmarsson & Johansson, 2003).

The result is that despite the availability of support programs for the rural small and medium enterprises, businesses located in the peripheral regions frequently do not take advantage of them.

This situation, in which demand does not meet supply, is relatively more common in rural areas of lesser-developed peripheral regions. This is true in the areas that are in greater need of assistance from the public system, where the alternatives offered by the private market are extremely meager (Bennett, Robson, & Bratton, 2001). The SMEs in these regions are located relatively far from the service centers and concentrations of economic activity. There is a lack of information regarding assistance programs in these regions, as well as a lack of awareness of their importance.

The relatively difficult economic situation in the periphery leads to a situation where the businesses are smaller and less innovative, often focusing on niche-markets (Lowe et al., 2000) and dealing more with immediate issues than with the problems essential to their functioning.

All of the factors described above make the phenomenon of discrepancy between supply and demand relatively more common in rural areas, particularly in lesser-developed peripheral regions.

The "Consultancy Program for Small- and Medium-Sized Enterprises" proposes a different approach, which may contribute to the solution of these constraints, instead of just offering a supply of support (consultancy and training) services to the SMEs and waiting for their demand for help.

The program was operated by means of consultants sent to the place of business to help identify the problems and define the type of consulting necessary. This type of program leads to an increase in the benefit-cost ratio through a more efficient identification of the main problems and needs. This approach of a diagnosis intervention has been found efficient in increasing the added value of existing business support programs in disadvantaged areas.

This program is not therefore intended to replace any existing support program of training or consultancy: on the contrary, it is intended to complement such programs and increase their added value, by adding the missing link between the SMEs and the supplied programs, contributing in this way to the solution of the existing market failure. The regional character of this program also contributes to the creation of an economic and social network in the region, facilitating a more efficient global development.

3. THE PROGRAM STRUCTURE

The program consists of:

1. A "reach out" approach, where the consultants go to the firm and offer their services.

2. A diagnostic holistic approach, where the consultant does not necessarily respond to the specific demands of the entrepreneur but rather helps him in the analysis of the functioning of the firm, trying to identify the main problems that put a constraint on the competitive ability of the firm.
3. Such "Consultancy" support is provided within the enterprise, through sessions of 2–3 h each, up to a total of about 15 h.

At the end of this stage, the consultant may be in a position to recommend to the entrepreneur the participation in specific support programs in most relevant fields (marketing, management, etc.) as identified in this stage or the continuation of the individual Consultancy Program in specific issues.

The program was conducted as part of the Sao Jose Project, targeted at the diminution of poverty in the rural area and implemented by the Secretary of Rural Development and SEBRAE, and guided by a steering committee.

3.1. Organizational Structure

3.1.1. Executive Committee (EC)

The Consultancy Program is directed by an EC of four Secretaries of the Government of Ceara: Rural Development, Agriculture, Labor, and Industrial Entrepreneurship, and the president of SEBRAE, a national public consultancy and training company. The EC meets at least once a month and discusses reports about the advancement of the Consultancy Program. All major decisions about the implementation of the program are taken by the EC.

3.1.2. Program Director (PD)

The PD is directly responsible for the implementation of the program, and for continuous follow-up and evaluation of the activities taken in the program. He is in charge of controlling both the financial aspects and the professional aspects of the program, and ensures that all actions are in concordance with the guidelines of the EC. The PD is also responsible for the realization of the feed-back questionnaire from the entrepreneurs (as will be described later).

3.1.3. Field Coordinators (FC)

A Field Coordinator (FC) is nominated for each region, in which the Consultancy Program is implemented. The FC is responsible for the application of the program in his/her region. The FC can also be considered a Master Consultant, who has a broad knowledge and experience in a wide range of issues. He should provide professional support and supervision to all consultants acting in the region, and take decisions about allocation or transfer of consultants between the firms. He is nominated by the consulting agency, basically SEBRAE, and reports to it and to the PC.

3.1.4. Consultants (C)

The Consultants work directly with the businesses and then report to the FC. A pool of consultants is built by the FC and kept in the files of the program. Consultants participate in a training program especially geared toward the needs of the Consultancy Program.

In a schematic way:

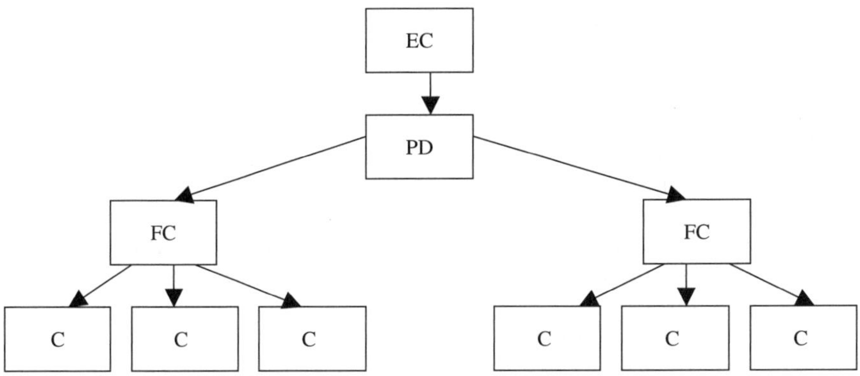

3.2. Steps in the Implementation of the Program

1. Take decision about a selected region for the implementation of the program, by the EC.
2. Prepare a listing of the SMEs in the region:

   This is done by the PD and the FC. The list includes basic information for each of the SMEs: branch, location, and number of workers.

3. Selecting SMEs to be assisted:

   This is done by the EC, using the following criteria:
   - Size: Small enterprises with 2–40 workers.
   - Branch: Higher priority to agro-businesses.
   - Enterprises with greater regional multiplier effect.
   - Located in a region with a regional office of the Secretariat of Local and Regional Development.
   - High growth potential.
4. Application of a preliminary questionnaire to SMEs to be assisted:

   By the Consultants, with the supervision of the FC. The questionnaire basically provides preliminary information about the firm and about the evaluation of the entrepreneur regarding the problems he faces.
5. Up to 15 h Diagnostic Consultancy program:

   By the Consultants with the supervision of the FC, on the premises of the firm based on sessions of 2–3 h each, with the objective of identifying the main problems of the firm, trying to solve them whenever possible and reaching a clear diagnosis. Guidelines for Diagnostic Consultancy should be followed:
   - The consultant should read the introduction of the preliminary questionnaire to the entrepreneur and make sure that it is understood by him.
   - Before any intervention, the consultant should assist the entrepreneur in completing the questionnaire.
   - The main objective of the 15 h consultancy is to reach a diagnosis of the situation of the business, support the entrepreneur in finding solutions whenever this is possible, and guiding him or her for further actions to be taken if any.
   - Consultancy is provided in sessions of 2–3 h each, on the premises of the firm. Those sessions are dedicated to learning the business, analyzing the problems together with the owner, trying to find solutions to some of them. A maximum of 15 h are allocated for this purpose.
   - The consultant and the owner should be aware of the fact that he may need another consultant who is more oriented toward the needs of his business. If this is the case, this should be reported to the FC, who would provide for another consultant.
   - At the end of the consulting process, the consultant is expected:
     a. To identify the major problems of the firm.
     b. To recommend actions that can be taken immediately by the owner to solve or reduce his problems.
     c. To recommend fields of consultancy or training that could be beneficial to the owner and that are offered within the region.

   d. In addition or alternatively, to recommend the continuation of the Consultancy Program for up to 85 h on the premises of the business, with a partial payment by the owner.

6. Report writing on Diagnostic Consultancy:

   By Consultants, submitted to FC and to PD. The report should include a technical section (dates of visits, hours, etc.), a diagnosis of the firm (including main problems to be treated), and a set of recommendations including alternatives for continuing treatment: end of intervention, use of specific programs offered in the region, or continuation of Consultancy on an 85 h basis.

7. Subjective evaluation by entrepreneur:

   By PD, based on a questionnaire given to each entrepreneur, who received a Diagnostic Consultancy. The questionnaire should not be applied by the consultants but by interviewers, directed by the PD. It would include questions about the degree of satisfaction of the entrepreneur from the support he received and the contribution of this program to the firm.

The information from the three questionnaires above (preliminary, diagnostic, evaluation) is coded and entered into a data base. This data base is the core component for the ongoing evaluation of the program.

4. IMPLEMENTATION

The program started in a small scale as a pilot project in 2001 in three regions: Ibiapaba, Quixeramobim, and Baixo Jaguaribe, and later expanded to three more regions: Sertao Central, Centro Sul, and Vale de Acarau.

The total number of businesses that participated in the program during the three years is 2,093. The average size of these businesses in terms of employees is 8.1. Approximately two-thirds of them are in industrial processing activities, some in artisan activity (17%), some in agriculture (9%), and the rest (9%) in other activities.

Most inputs (75%) used by the businesses, come from the region in which they are located and most of the production is sold within the region (71%). Still, there are some relationships with other regions in the state (16% of inputs and output), and even with other places outside the State of Ceara (9% of inputs, 13% of output).

The analysis of the findings supported our hypothesis about the existence of a market failure in the operation of the existing programs and the necessity of this program. It appears that practically all of the businesses that participated in the program faced difficulties and need consulting in a variety of areas but never had access to such public support, and therefore missed the opportunity to contribute to regional development, and to increase employment and income in their community.

A large majority of the businesses face problems in a variety of fields:

- Over 75% in financing, management, marketing.
- Over 50% in planning, layout, technology.
- Over 33% in human resources and accounting.
- About 20% in transportation and infrastructure.

Most of them encounter problems in more than one field. One-third of the businesses were evaluated by the consultants as being close to the point of collapse. However, despite the fact that these businesses were in need of these services and despite the existence of a varied supply of existing services, two-thirds of the businesses assisted through this program had not previously received any type of assistance. For almost two-thirds of them the reason for this was specifically because of the long distance involved. Only 1% specified cost as a factor.

One of the important contributions of the program is that it assists the entrepreneurs in correctly identifying their problems and subsequently their achievements are improved. A preliminary analysis of the results of this program (Schwartz & Bar-El, 2004), based on the pilot phase, shows an important contribution to the ability of the entrepreneurs to correctly identify and rank their problems. It also helped the entrepreneurs change their course of thinking, from attaching great importance to external factors beyond their control, such as labor force and infrastructure to factors that they can change such as marketing and particularly management. It was found that for each case of identification of a problem the chances for a false identification are 43%, which is not very far from the expected 50% probability in case of a random identification. Most of the mistakes are of the "false-negative" type; defined as the lack of awareness of existing problems (the business owner fails to identify existing problems in given aspects of his activity such as marketing, management). Other mistakes are of the "false-positive" type, where the business owner finds problems where they do not actually exist.

The entrepreneurs were asked to rank their satisfaction with the program and its contribution to the business development. The results show that most of the businesses expressed a high level of satisfaction with the program. More than two-thirds of the businesses assessed that the program did improve their situation.

Relating to major relevant fields of influence, a large majority attributed a high grade (8–10, out of a maximum 10) to the contribution of the consultancy in better identifying the needs of the market, increasing growth, improving technology, decreasing costs, and increasing income. The average level of satisfaction with the program as a whole expressed by the businesses is 8.5.

These findings show that the program improves the capabilities of the businesses in the interior by giving them the tools to increase their productivity and their competitivity, and enables them to integrate into the national economic growth process. In the words of one of the entrepreneurs: "We feel that we can do something for ourselves and that we are part of this nation."

5. CONCLUSION

We can conclude by saying that the results of the Consultancy Program for SMEs show that there is need for such a program in the interior. The program improved the small businesses' capabilities, increased their competitiveness, and aided in their development.

The findings show that there is a market failure in the interior regarding the existing support programs for SMEs in the interior, and that the Consultancy Program bridges this gap by providing the missing link. It seems that despite the existence of a varied supply of assistance services for SMEs, and despite the fact that these businesses are in need of the business services, most of the businesses that were approached by the program had not previously received any type of assistance.

The program is adapted to the specific characteristics and needs of the small and medium rural enterprises, and helps them in strengthening their competitiveness and their productivity, and also enables them to integrate into the process of national economic growth. Since entrepreneurship and small- and medium-sized businesses are important components for economic growth, the program actually assists in strengthening the local economic capabilities of the interior, decreases unemployment, and contributes to increasing income. The increased ability of the enterprises to compete in the wider regional market enables them to integrate into the global economy of the state, instead of remaining focused on local demand.

The continuation of this program on a permanent basis and its expansion into other regions, taking into consideration the changes that are needed may add a substantive contribution to the economic growth of the interior and to the income of the local population, and therefore to a substantive reduction of poverty and inequality while at the same time making an important contribution to the economic growth of the state as a whole.

REFERENCES

Bartlett, W., & Bukvic, V. (2001). Barriers to SME growth in Slovenia. *MOCT-MOST*, *11*, 177–195.

Bennett, R. J., Bratton, W., & Robson, P. J. (2000). Business advice: The influence of distance. *Regional Studies*, *34*(9), 813–828.

Bennett, R. J., Robson, P. J., & Bratton, W. J. (2001). The influence of location on the use by SMEs of external advice and collaboration. *Urban Studies*, *38*(9), 1531–1557.

Binks, M. (1979). Finance for expansion in the small firm. *Lloyds Bank Review*, *157*, 32–43.

Chrisman, J. (1999). The influence of outsider-generated knowledge resources on venture creation. *Journal of Small Business Management*, *37*(3), 42–58.

Clark, D., Berkeley, N., & Steuer, N. (2001). Research note: Attitudes to growth among owners of small and medium-sized enterprises and the implications for business advice: Some evidence from the clothing industry in coventry. *International Small Business Journal*, *19*(3), 72–77.

Curran, J., & Blackburn, R. (2000). Panacea or white elephant? A critical examination of the proposed new small business service and response to the DTI consultancy paper. In: J. Mawson (Ed.), *Policy Review Section, Regional Studies*, *34*(2), 181–189.

Deakins, D. (1999). *Entrepreneurship and small firms*. London: McGraw-Hill Publishing Company.

Devins, D. (1999). Research note: Supporting established micro businesses: Policy issues emerging from an evaluation. *International Small Business Journal*, *1*, 86–96.

Felsenstein, D., & Schwartz, D. (1993). Constraints on small business development across the life cycle. *Entrepreneurship and Regional Development*, *5*, 227–245.

Gelderen, V. M., Frese, M., & Thurik, R. (2000). Strategies, uncertainty and performance of small business startups. *Small Business Economics*, *15*, 165–181.

Gibb, A. A. (1997). Small firms' training and competitiveness: Building upon the small business as a learning organization. *International Small Business Journal*, *15*(3), 13–29.

Henderson, R., Sutherland, J., & Turley, S. (2000). Management development in small business: A sub-regional examination of practice, expectation and experience. *Regional Studies*, *34*(1), 81–86.

Hjalmarsson, D., & Johansson, A. W. (2003). Public advisory services – Theory and practice. *Entrepreneurship and Regional Development*, *15*, 83–98.

Huang, X., & Brown, A. (1999). An analysis and classification of problems in small business. *International Small Business Journal*, *18*(1), 73–85.

Leite, P. S. (1986). *Forces that will shape future rural development: Northeast Brazil's case*. Fortaleza: Federal University of Ceara.

Liedholm, C. (2002). Small business dynamics: Evidence from Africa and Latin America. *Small Business Economics, 18*(13), 227–242.
Low, M. B., & Abrahamson, E. (1997). Movements, bandwagons, and clones: Industry evolution and the entrepreneurial process. *Journal of Business Venturing, 12*(6), 435–458.
Lowe, P., Talbot, H., & Hannon, P. (2000). Policy for small business support in rural areas: A critical assessment of proposals for the small business service. *Regional Studies, 34*(5), 479–487.
North, D., & Smallbone, D. (2000). Innovative activity in SMEs and rural economic development: Some evidence from England. *European Planning Studies, 8*(1), 87–106.
Patton, D., Marlow, S., & Hannon, P. (2000). The relationship between training and small firm performance: Research frameworks and lost quests. *International Small Business Journal, 19*(1), 11–27.
Ren, W. (1999). US government information need, awareness, and searching: A study of small business executives. *Journal of Government Information, 26*(5), 453–465.
Rothwell, R., & Dodgson, M. (1991). External linkages and innovation in small and medium sized enterprises. *R&D Management, 21*, 125–137.
Schwartz, D., & Bar-El, R. (2004). Targeted consultancy services as an instrument for the development of remote SMEs-a Brazilian case. *International Small Business Journal, 22*(5), 497–513.
Smallbone, D., & Welter, F. (2001). The distinctiveness of entrepreneurship in transition economies. *Small Business Economics, 16*, 249–262.
Tendler, J., & Amorim, M. A. (1996). Small firms and their helpers: Lessons on demand. *World Development, 24*(3), 407–426.
Townroe, P. J., & Mallalieu, K. (1990). Entrepreneurial roles and entrepreneurial competence in regional economic development, small business research program. ESCR Small Business Research Initiative, London.
UNCTAD-United Nations Conference on Trade and Development. (2000). Development strategies and support services for SMEs: Proceedings of four intergovernmental expert meetings, United Nations, New York.
Westhead, P., & Storey, D. (1996). Management training and firm performance: Why is the link so weak? *International Small Business Journal, 14*(4), 13–24.
Winders, R. (2000). Small business development and non-metropolitan job growth in Georgia. *Growth and Change, 31*(1), 82–107.

PART V
POLICY RESULTS

CHAPTER 11

POSITIVE SIGNS IN THE NEW DEVELOPMENT TRENDS OF CEARA

The governments of Ceara in the last decade or two have certainly shown clear signs of preoccupation with the problems of poverty and inequality, without losing sight of the need for economic growth of the state as a whole. For many years, the policies adopted by the governments as described above have been strongly oriented on one hand on the attraction of investments for the achievement of healthy macroeconomic growth, and on the other hand on the solution of acute problems of development in the interior of the state, such as support to agricultural development, heavy investments in education and infrastructures, and increasing access of the population to land and finance. At the beginning of the new millennium, the governments have structured their policy approach in a clear model based on the premise that the problems of inequality and poverty are to a large extent a result of a market failure: the lack of appropriate adaptation of the demographic and social changes to major structural economic changes (the diminution of the weight of agriculture in the economy). The policy elements that were structured and strengthened are therefore the spatial reorganization of the state (supporting the growth of urban centers outside the metropolitan area), provision of support to local economic activities in their efforts to respond to local market failures (by improving access to technology, finance, professional services, and education facilities), and encouragement of the building of a regional social capital by supporting regional organization and cooperation, and participation of all parts of the society in the development process.

The results of such types of policies are not always easy to identify. Some of these specific policy measures provide positive results only after a decade or two (such as the restructuring of the urban system). However, statistical data on the main indicators of development of the State of Ceara (CE) provide at least some positive signs of trends of diminution of inequality and poverty, compared with the whole Northeast (NE) region and Brazil. We relate to the analysis done in a previous chapter comparing the years between 1992 and 2004, try to check if such changes are more accentuated in the years since the beginning of the new millennium and changes in some indicators of internal gaps in Ceara between the rural interior and the urban center. Results for the whole period from 1992 to 2004, especially when compared with the NE and Brazil, can certainly provide a good evaluation of the efficiency of the policy of the governments of Ceara since the nineties. The influence of the new measures started at the beginning of the new millennium may be harder to test because of the time lag before which their impact is visible.

1. ECONOMIC GROWTH

Before anything else, it is important to call attention to the fact indicated above that the economic growth of the CE does not lag behind the nation as a whole. Although the average GDP growth rate was on average somewhat lower in Ceara for the period from 1992 to 2005 (2.6% compared with 2.8%), the beginning of the millennium shows a more rapid growth in Ceara: between 2002 and 2005, the average growth rate of the economy in Ceara increased to 2.9% a year, while the GDP of Brazil grew at the much lower rate of 2.4% per year. This growth of the economy of the CE was accompanied by a rapid growth in exports and an improvement in the balance of payments, indicating a process of integration in the global economy. Although the growth rate of the economy of Ceara is not very high, its trend is not lower than that of the nation as a whole, and therefore we can state that if any process of diminution of poverty and inequality has happened during this period, it is important to recognize that it did not happen at the expense of a decreasing macroeconomic growth.

2. CHANGING ECONOMIC STRUCTURE, ADAPTED BY A CHANGING DEMOGRAPHIC STRUCTURE

The economic growth of Ceara in the last few years has been characterized, as expected, by a changing structure, with a relative decrease in the weight

Table 1. Distribution of Employed Workers Aged 10 and Over by Sector of Main Economic Activity and by Region, 1999 and 2004.

Economic Sector	Ceara		Northeast		Brazil	
	1999	2004	1999	2004	1999	2004
Total	100%	100%	100%	100%	100%	100%
Agriculture	40%	31%	41%	36%	24%	21%
Manufacturing and construction	14%	21%	14%	15%	20%	21%
Services and others	46%	48%	45%	49%	56%	58%

Source: Elaboration of data from PNAD 1999 and 2004; see IBGE (Various years).

of agriculture and an increase in the weight of industry. The following table shows that this changing structure has been much more salient in Ceara than it was in the NE as a developing region or Brazil as a whole (Table 1).

The following main features characterize the changing structure of the economy of Ceara:

1. The share of agriculture in employment has drastically decreased since the end of the previous millennium, from 40 to 31% in Ceara. Parallely, the share of industry and construction in employment increased significantly from 14 to 21%. This process was not as clear and significant in the developing region of the NE: the share of agriculture decreased there at a much smaller rate, and that of industry and construction hardly changed.
2. In the same period between 1999 and 2004, the process of urbanization continued, and the share of rural population out of total population decreased from 33 to 24% (9% less in 2004 than 1999, equal to the diminution of employment).
3. At the same time, the share of agriculture in product stabilized at about 6–7% after a continuous decrease as shown above.

We find here, therefore, signs of a quite healthy process of economic growth, with a stable production of agricultural products, relatively fewer workers, and a process of migration of proportional shares of rural population to urban places. Producing the same relative quantities of agricultural products with fewer workers directly implies the existence of a process of increasing productivity in the rural area.

3. DECREASING RURAL/URBAN GAPS

Assessing the changes that occurred in the rural/urban gaps that were found above for the year 1999, we find an important improvement, in absolute terms and in comparison with the NE and Brazil. The following table provides data on average income levels for various groups of population and calculated rural/urban gaps.

Data for income in 1999 and 2004 in the rural and urban spaces are shown in Table 2. The income data are not in real terms, and there is therefore no sense in testing income growth (this will be done at a later stage with real income data). We focus here on the ratio between the income of rural and urban populations. Results show signs of quite interesting phenomena. Beginning with the end of the table, we see that the ratio between rural and urban workers with an income increased slightly from

Table 2. Average Monthly Income and Gaps in Ceara, Northeast, Southeast, and Brazil, by Population Groups, 1999 and 2004 ($R and Indicators).

Years	Ceara		Northeast		Brazil	
	1999	2004	1999	2004	1999	2004
All persons aged 10 and over						
Total	172	270	177	279	313	474
Rural	74	127	96	143	138	230
Urban	218	313	221	331	355	522
Gaps indicator						
Rural/urban	0.34	0.41	0.43	0.43	0.39	0.44
Economically active population (EAP)						
Total	234	361	246	377	445	647
Rural	90	151	123	176	180	294
Urban	322	434	329	466	523	727
Gaps indicator						
Rural/urban	0.28	0.35	0.37	0.38	0.34	0.40
EAP with income						
Total	314	432	334	465	552	758
Rural	149	204	197	245	275	404
Urban	387	500	404	548	615	824
Gaps indicator						
Rural/urban	0.39	0.41	0.49	0.45	0.45	0.49

Source: Microdata on PNAD 1999 and 2004; see IBGE (various years).

1999 to 2004: rural income was 39% of urban income in 1999, and this ratio grew to 41% in 2004. This ratio is still lower than that of the NE, but we can see that the whole NE region has experienced a growing gap between the rural and urban population during this period (the gap for the nation as a whole decreased substantively).

The most interesting finding is the very substantive decrease of the gap between rural and urban spaces regarding the economically active population, meaning the population of workers with the addition of the unemployed labor force and workers with no remuneration. The ratio was 28% in 1999, and it grew to 35% in 2004, much more than in the NE and Brazil. Consequently, we also find a very substantive diminution of the gap between the rural and urban population of all persons aged 10 years and over. In the NE specifically there was no improvement at all in this indicator, and Brazil the improvement was smaller.

The picture presented by these data is that during the period between 1999 and 2004 the income per worker in the rural area increased slightly more than the income of the worker in the urban area, but most of the improvement and decrease of inequality between the two sectors is due to the fact that an increasing number of unemployed and non-remunerated workers joined the group of workers with income. This is a quite clear sign of decreasing hidden or open unemployment in the rural area, and therefore a sign of increasing productivity.

4. DECREASING METROPOLITAN/INTERIOR GAPS

The decreasing gaps between the rural and urban population reflect changes in two dimensions: decreasing gaps between the metropolitan area (mostly urban) and interior, and also decreasing gaps between the rural and urban population in the interior itself. Taking the indicators for those gaps as shown for 1999 in Chapter 2, Table 5, we compare them with data for 2004 in Table 3.

Again, we see a similar phenomenon as the one described above. For the labor force that is employed in a paying job, the gap between the interior and MRF (Metropolitan Region of Fortaleza) did not decrease and even increased slightly: on the average, working persons had an increase in their income at more or less the same rate in the interior and MRF, so that the paid workers in the interior gained 45% of the income of the MRF workers. However, as seen in the table, significant effect was due to the inclusion of unemployed and non-remunerated workers into the group of the paid

Table 3. Average Monthly Income in Ceara, by Population Groups, 2004 ($R and Indicators).

	Average Monthly Income ($R) and Gaps	
	1999	2004
All persons aged 10 and over		
Total	172	270
MRF	258	390
Interior	115	183
Rural in interior	74	125
Urban in interior	162	218
Gaps indicators		
Interior/MRF	0.44	0.47
Rural/urban in interior	0.46	0.57
EAP		
Total	234	361
MRF	386	549
Interior	148	235
Rural in interior	90	147
Urban in interior	232	297
Gaps indicators		
Interior/MRF	0.38	0.43
Rural/urban in interior	0.39	0.49
EAP with income		
Total	314	432
MRF	459	637
Interior	215	288
Rural in interior	149	200
Urban in interior	286	340
Gaps indicators		
Interior/MRF	0.47	0.45
Rural/urban in interior	0.52	0.59

Source: Microdata on PNAD Ceara 1999 and 2004; see IBGE (Various years).

workers. The gap between the average income of the economically active population in the interior and that of MRF decreased at a very substantive rate: instead of 38%, the average income ratio increased to 43%. It can also be seen that an important dimension of the decreasing gap is the diminution of the gap between the rural and urban population within the interior itself.

We detect therefore some interesting signs of a process of inclusion of inactive or inefficient labor force in the interior into the group of economically active workers who gain an income for their work, and this process is stronger amongst the rural population. There is also probably a process of increasing average income of the working labor force with income, although it may not be fully visible at this time because this average may be biased due to the relatively lower income of the workers who recently joined this group. This is shown in the next section.

5. INCREASING INCOME LEVELS AND INCLUSION OF NON-REMUNERATED WORKERS

The increasing productivity-level is also shown by an improving picture of remuneration for work. In our analysis in a previous chapter, we show two indicators as a sign of low-levels of productivity: the share of workers with an income of one minimum salary or less, and the share of unpaid workers, who may actually hide unemployment. Since 1999, these two indicators show a significant positive change in Ceara, as compared with the NE and Brazil as a whole. Comparative results are shown in the following tables (Tables 4a and 4b).

The share of paid workers who gained up to one minimum salary decreased from 50% in 1999 to 46% in 2004. This is quite similar to the decrease in the NE, but greater than that of the whole nation. Still, the income level in Ceara is relatively low and a serious gap with the nation has to be closed or at least diminished.

The share of unpaid workers out of total workers made much more significant progress: it went down from 25% in 1999 to 18% in 2004. This decrease is greater than in the NE and nation.

The signs shown by those data are that the main improvement in the remuneration of workers is the fact that fewer of them work without being paid (or are disguised unemployed), many begin working for a salary, but the increase of the level of salaries is not yet very high.

Table 4a. Percent of Occupied Workers with up to 1 Minimum Salary, out of Total Occupied Workers with an Income, 1999 and 2004.

Ceara		Northeast		Brazil	
1999	2004	1999	2004	1999	2004
50%	46%	48%	43%	24%	22%

Source: Elaboration of data from PNAD 1999 and 2004.

Table 4b. Percent of Unpaid Occupied Workers out of Total Occupied Workers, 1999 and 2004.

Ceara		Northeast		Brazil	
1999	2004	1999	2004	1999	2004
25%	18%	24%	20%	14%	11%

Source: Elaboration of data from PNAD 1999 and 2004.

6. DECREASING GAPS IN EDUCATIONAL LEVELS

From this section on, we use historical data from IPEA, beginning in 1981, to try and detect differences in trends between the development of the CE, compared with the NE, and nation as a whole (BR). We take four anchor points for comparison: 1981, 1992, 1999, and 2004. For each indicator we compare the values in CE, NE, and BR, calculate the changing ratio between CE and NE and between CE and BR, and annual rate of improvement (in the sense of decreasing gaps between CE and NE or BR) for each indicator.

Beginning with education, we measure changes by using three main indicators: the rate of illiteracy for the adult population 15 years old or older, the rate of illiteracy for the population of ages 10–14, which would be more indicative of the results of appropriate education policies, and average schooling years of the population 25 years old or older.

The changes in illiteracy rate of population aged 15 or older already shows interesting results (Table 5).

The illiteracy rates decrease continuously during the whole period everywhere – in Ceara, the NE, and Brazil. However, the important question here is the relative rate of decrease. The illiteracy rate of the population aged 15 years or older was about 42% in 1981 in Ceara and the NE, 1.86 times more than the average illiteracy rate of Brazil. During the years, the illiteracy rate decreased in all places, but till 1999 it decreased on average at a lower annual rate (calculated as the geometric mean of percent change in the illiteracy rate) in Ceara (1.9% till 1992 and 3.0% till 1999) and the NE (2.1 and 2.9%, respectively) than Brazil (2.5 and 3.6%, respectively), leading to an increasing gap between Ceara and Brazil. However, during the last few years since the beginning of the new millennium, we find a drastic improvement in Ceara, where the illiteracy rate has been decreasing at an annual rate of 4.7%, much more than that of the NE (3.4%)

Table 5. Illiteracy Rates of Population Aged 15 Years or Over.

	1981	1992	1999	2004
CE	42.4	34.5	27.8	21.8
NE	41.6	32.8	26.6	22.4
BR	22.8	17.2	13.3	11.4
CE/NE	1.02	1.05	1.05	0.97
CE/BR	1.86	2.01	2.09	1.91
Average annual improvement rate				
CE		−1.9%	−3.0%	−4.7%
NE		−2.1%	−2.9%	−3.4%
BR		−2.5%	−3.6%	−3.0%

Source: IPEA data.

and Brazil (3.0%). As a consequence, the gap between Ceara and Brazil decreased significantly, although it is still quite high (1.91), and for the first time, the illiteracy rate in Ceara is lower than the average of the NE.

While the illiteracy rate in Ceara is still very high despite the significant improvement, we should remember that decreasing illiteracy is achieved mostly by policies oriented toward the youngest population. Solving illiteracy amongst the older population is quite difficult and may also be less cost-efficient. Decreasing illiteracy amongst youngsters is a most important investment in future development. We therefore analyze in the next table the changes in illiteracy for the population aged 10–14 (Table 6).

Results here are much more striking. The situation in Ceara in 1982 was much worse than Brazil (2.42 times greater share of illiterate kids aged 10–14 in Ceara than Brazil), and the rate of improvement was about the same till 1999 (during the nineties a very strong decrease of illiteracy in youngsters was observed overall at a rate of more than 10% a year): in spite of a sharp decrease in illiteracy rates, the gap between Ceara and Brazil remained almost unchanged. A very drastic improvement occurred in the new millennium, when the progress made by Ceara was much greater than in the NE and Brazil: while in the NE and Brazil illiteracy continued decreasing at the same rate as in the past or less, Ceara made a major move by achieving an annual improvement of 16.4%. The gap in the illiteracy rate of youngsters in Ceara compared with Brazil is now much lower than that of the past (1.39 times higher instead of 2.42 in the past). Compared to the NE, Ceara had the same illiteracy rate during the nineties, but is now in a much better situation, with a rate of illiteracy that reaches only two-thirds of that of the NE.

Table 6. Illiteracy Rates of Population Aged 10–14 Years.

	1981	1992	1999	2004
CE	47.6	28.9	13.0	5.3
NE	41.8	29.1	12.7	8.0
BR	19.7	12.4	5.5	3.8
CE/NE	1.14	0.99	1.02	0.66
CE/BR	2.42	2.33	2.36	1.39
Average annual improvement rate				
CE		−4.4%	−10.8%	−16.4%
NE		−3.2%	−11.2%	−8.8%
BR		−4.1%	−11.0%	−7.1%

Source: IPEA data.

Table 7. Average Years of Schooling of the Population Aged 25 and Older.

	1981	1992	1999	2004
CE	2.3	3.4	4.0	4.9
NE	2.5	3.5	4.2	4.9
BR	3.9	4.9	5.7	6.4
CE/NE	0.93	0.97	0.96	1.00
CE/BR	0.59	0.69	0.71	0.77
Average annual improvement rate				
CE		3.6%	2.3%	4.1%
NE		3.1%	2.6%	3.1%
BR		2.1%	2.2%	2.3%

Source: IPEA data.

A frequently used indicator for the evaluation of the human capital is the average number of years of schooling of the adult population. The changes in this indicator for the population aged 25 and older, shown in Table 7, reinforces the conclusions reached above: a substantive leap of the CE in the first years of the new millennium, leading to a clear diminution of gaps.

Again, we find an improvement in the level of education overall, but the most important measure is actually the relative rate of change. During the two decades of the eighties and nineties, the educational-level of the population of Ceara was lower than that of the NE and Brazil, but we detected a slight but continuous diminution of gaps. The most striking change happened in the last years, when the improvement of the human capital in Ceara occurred at a much higher annual rate (4.1%) than in the NE (3.1%) and Brazil (2.3%). In 2004, Ceara had already closed the gap with the NE and substantively diminished with Brazil: the average number of schooling years in Ceara (4.9 years) reaches now 77% of the Brazilian average (6.4 years). Despite this very substantive advance, it should be noted that the average number of schooling years is still very low in Ceara and Brazil, and much work has still to be done to achieve the acceptable levels.

7. INCREASING PER CAPITA HOUSEHOLD INCOME

The changing economic structure, improving balance between the rural and urban area, improving balance between the MRF and interior, increasing level of education of the population, all these lead to an apparent diminution in the gaps of income per capita between Ceara and the NE and Brazil. A previous chapter has already shown the diminution of such gaps in relation to the family income, from 1992 to 2004. We present here the data from IPEA on the changes in per capita household income between the four time points, in real terms of 2001 Reais (Table 8).

According to the IPEA data, per capita household income in real terms has slightly decreased from 1981 to 1992 but at a lower rate in Ceara, increased between 1992 and 1999 but at a higher rate in Ceara, and slightly decreased from 1999 to 2004 in the NE and Brazil but not in Ceara. Consequently, these data show a process of decreasing gaps, where Ceara, which had always a lower income than the NE, closed this gap in the last few years, and diminished the gap with Brazil, again, mostly in the last few years.

Table 8. Household Income Per Capita, in 2001 Reais.

	1981	1992	1999	2004
CE	171	156	207	208
NE	177	162	212	206
BR	285	256	326	313
CE/NE	0.97	0.96	0.98	1.01
CE/BR	0.60	0.61	0.63	0.66
Average annual improvement rate				
CE		−0.8%	4.1%	0.1%
NE		−0.8%	3.9%	−0.6%
BR		−1.0%	3.5%	−0.8%

Source: IPEA data.

8. POVERTY DIMINUTION

The increasing levels of income and education as described above may not necessarily lead to the diminution of poverty-levels. However, the policy adopted by the CE, focusing on regional development and the solution of market failures that prevent the advance of poor regions and populations, is also expected to produce results in the field of poverty and inequality. Positive results in this field are expected as a consequence of changes that have been shown in the various issues above: adaptation of agriculture employment, decreasing illiteracy amongst the lowest classes, improvements in human capital.

We use here the familiar measures of poverty and indigent poverty as defined by IPEA (slightly different from the figures provided by IBGE as described in the chapter above). As in previous sections, we compare the figures of Ceara with results in the NE and Brazil, and detect changes in the gaps between them (Tables 9 and 10).

The reduction of poverty-levels in Brazil as a whole did not begin before 1992. In fact, the first significant drop in the statistics of poverty-levels happened in 1995. This may be the result of some changes in definitions or measurements, but since we use comparative indicators, the impact of such changes may not be significant.

After 1992, the decrease in poverty-levels occurs, but at quite a slow pace. Till 1999, poverty-levels decrease even more slowly in Ceara and the whole of NE than Brazil, causing an increase in poverty gaps. However, in the last few years between 1999 and 2004, Ceara shows a faster rate of

Table 9. Poverty-Levels (Shares of Population under the Poverty Line).

	1981	1992	1999	2004
CE	0.730	0.683	0.612	0.572
NE	0.679	0.678	0.606	0.578
BR	0.409	0.422	0.353	0.336
CE/NE	1.08	1.01	1.01	0.99
CE/BR	1.78	1.62	1.73	1.70
Average annual improvement rate				
CE		−0.6%	−1.6%	−1.3%
NE		0.0%	−1.6%	−0.9%
BR		0.3%	−2.5%	−1.0%

Source: IPEA data.

Table 10. Indigent Poverty-Levels.

	1981	1992	1999	2004
CE	0.443	0.433	0.319	0.264
NE	0.359	0.401	0.310	0.280
BR	0.173	0.200	0.150	0.131
CE/NE	1.23	1.08	1.03	0.94
CE/BR	2.56	2.17	2.13	2.02
Average annual improvement rate				
CE		−0.2%	−4.3%	−3.7%
NE		1.0%	−3.6%	−2.0%
BR		1.3%	−4.0%	−2.7%

Source: IPEA data.

decrease of poverty, closing the gap with the NE and reducing it with Brazil to 1.70.

A clearer picture is shown by the data on indigent poverty: extreme poverty was always a very painful problem in Ceara, with greater rates than the NE and more than twice the rates in Brazil. After 1992 those rates decreased in Ceara at the same rate they decreased in Brazil, thus keeping the same gap, but in the last few years the decrease in indigent poverty rates was much greater in Ceara (3.7% a year) than Brazil (2.7%) and the NE (2.0%). The indigence poverty rate in Ceara is still very high (26.4% in 2004), but today for the first time it is lower than in the NE, and its gap with the rate in Brazil has decreased quite substantively.

9. DECREASING PROFUNDITY OF POVERTY

Poverty may have different depth-levels. The distinction between poverty and indigent poverty already provides an indication of the depth of poverty. As we saw in the previous section, the advance of the CE in the last few years in the reduction of poverty is good in comparison to the advancement in NE or Brazil, but the more important achievement of the policy of Ceara is the reduction of the profundity of poverty: people are somewhat less extremely poor. Another measure for the profundity of poverty may be the average level of income of the poor and indigent poor. The next tables show changes in this respect (Tables 11 and 12).

Again, we can see that there is progress, mostly in the last few years, in another dimension of poverty. The poor population (including the indigent

Table 11. Average Household Income Per Capita of the Poor Population.

	1981	1992	1999	2004
CE	49	45	53	58
NE	56	51	57	60
BR	62	59	62	65
CE/NE	0.87	0.88	0.93	0.97
CE/BR	0.78	0.77	0.86	0.89
Average annual improvement rate				
CE		−0.8%	2.4%	1.8%
NE		−0.8%	1.6%	1.0%
BR		−0.4%	0.7%	0.9%

Source: IPEA data.

Table 12. Average Household Income Per Capita of the Indigent Poor Population.

	1981	1992	1999	2004
CE	31	27	30	34
NE	34	30	34	35
BR	35	32	33	34
CE/NE	0.92	0.89	0.89	0.97
CE/BR	0.90	0.85	0.91	0.99
Average annual improvement rate				
CE		−1.2%	1.5%	2.5%
NE		−1.1%	1.8%	0.6%
BR		−0.8%	0.4%	0.6%

Source: IPEA data.

poor) in Ceara always had an average level of income much lower than that in the NE or Brazil. In other words, the poor in Ceara always were poorer than in the NE or Brazil. The improvement rate of this situation, mostly from 1999 to 2004, has been much stronger in Ceara than the NE and Brazil, especially in the case of the indigent poor. This has led to a situation where the profundity of poverty is more or less equal in Ceara to the NE or Brazil: the poor people in Ceara are today no longer poorer (especially true for the indigent poor) than in the NE or Brazil.

10. DECREASING INEQUALITY

Decreasing poverty does not of course necessarily mean a decreasing inequality. We use here a few frequently used indicators for inequality, again based on the IPEA data, and check the rate of change in Ceara compared with NE and Brazil (Tables 13–16).

All four indicators show that the process of diminution of inequality is actually quite recent, and began only in the new millennium. The Gini coefficient of inequality had an increasing trend in overall years till the end of the previous millennium, although generally the increasing trend was not as strong in Ceara. Since the beginning of the millennium, we find a decreasing trend of inequality, at a higher rate in Ceara than the NE and

Table 13. Gini Coefficients.

	1981	1992	1999	2004
CE	0.592	0.605	0.613	0.576
NE	0.571	0.593	0.605	0.583
BR	0.584	0.583	0.594	0.572
CE/NE	1.04	1.02	1.01	0.99
CE/BR	1.01	1.04	1.03	1.01
Average annual improvement rate				
CE		0.2%	0.2%	−1.2%
NE		0.3%	0.3%	−0.7%
BR		0.0%	0.3%	−0.8%

Source: IPEA data.

Table 14. Share of Income of 50% Poorest Population.

	1981	1992	1999	2004
CE	14.0	12.2	12.9	14.5
NE	14.9	13.0	13.0	14.1
BR	13.1	13.1	12.7	13.8
CE/NE	0.94	0.94	0.99	1.03
CE/BR	1.07	0.93	1.01	1.05
Average annual improvement rate				
CE		−1.2%	0.8%	2.4%
NE		−1.2%	0.0%	1.6%
BR		0.0%	−0.4%	1.7%

Source: IPEA data.

Table 15. Share of Income of 1% Richest Population.

	1981	1992	1999	2004
CE	17.2	15.8	17.7	15.2
NE	15.9	14.7	16.5	15.7
BR	12.7	13.2	13.2	13.0
CE/NE	1.08	1.07	1.07	0.97
CE/BR	1.35	1.20	1.34	1.17
Average annual improvement rate				
CE		−0.8%	1.6%	−3.0%
NE		−0.7%	1.7%	−1.0%
BR		0.4%	0.0%	−0.3%

Source: IPEA data.

Table 16. Ratio of Average Income of Richest 20% and Poorest 20% of Population.

	1981	1992	1999	2004
CE	19.7	30.3	26.6	19.5
NE	18.6	26.7	23.9	21.3
BR	23.6	26.4	26.4	22.4
CE/NE	1.06	1.14	1.11	0.92
CE/BR	0.83	1.15	1.01	0.87
Average annual improvement rate				
CE		4.0%	−1.8%	−6.0%
NE		3.3%	−1.6%	−2.3%
BR		1.0%	0.0%	−3.2%

Source: IPEA data.

Brazil: in 2004, Ceara almost reaches the Gini coefficient of Brazil, and for the first time has a lower Gini coefficient than the NE. This process is also apparent in the strongest decreasing income share of the 1% richest population, the strongest increase in the income share of the 50% poorest population, and the strongest decrease in the gap between the average income of the 20% richest and 20% poorest population.

11. CONCLUSION

The heavy problem faced by the CE in its development process is the same problem encountered by most developing countries and certainly by the

Brazilian states: how to solve the poverty problem and achieve a reduction of inequalities, without prejudicing the economic growth of the state. Literature and experience in other countries show, as demonstrated in a previous chapter, that economic growth tends to lead to growing inequalities, and direct social assistance to poorer segments of the population may inhibit the process of economic growth. The CE has adopted an approach based on the assessment that inequality in a process of economic growth may result from the emergence of market failures in the development of poorer regions. The analysis made in a previous chapter for the year 1999 actually indicates the existence of such market failures: the changing structure of the economy (decreasing weight of agriculture) is not met by appropriate adjustments in the demographic structure (spatial distribution of the population) and the social and organizational structures in regions outside the metropolis. The policy measures taken by the CE were therefore oriented toward the solution of such failures, using regional development as a major instrument for development with the reduction of poverty and inequality: urban spatial restructuring, regional organization, solution of market failures that prevent economic growth of local initiatives, etc., as described in detail in earlier chapters.

The measures taken by the CE from the nineties and policy structures implemented in the last few years since the beginning of the new millennium are expected to lead to the coexistence of economic growth, decreasing inequality, and decreasing poverty. It is hard to statistically prove such effects, especially given the fact that economic growth and development is also heavily influenced by policy measures at the national-level. The quantitative preliminary analysis presented above is therefore mostly based on comparative indicators for Ceara, the NE, and Brazil, for three time periods, based on the IPEA data: from 1981 to 1992, 1999, and 2004. The results show a quite encouraging picture about the path taken by the CE, in comparison with the whole region and country. In summary, the most important signs that appear from this analysis are the following:

1. Economic growth in Ceara is not significantly less than that of the NE or Brazil since 1981, but since the beginning of the millennium we find an average higher growth in Ceara than Brazil and the NE. Still, the rate of growth is not very impressive, and can certainly achieve much higher levels in the future.
2. The changing economic structure shown by the decreased relative weight of agriculture has been followed in the last few years much more than the past by an appropriate diminution of employment in this sector, and a

more significant process of urbanization. This process has occurred in Ceara much more successfully than the whole NE. This directly implies an increasing level of average productivity in the rural sector.

3. The gaps between the income of the rural and urban population that were detected in our diagnosis in 1999 significantly decreased till 2004. The gap has decreased in Ceara more than the NE as a whole. An important feature is that beyond the decrease of the gap for workers with an income, we find a much stronger decrease for the population of the whole active population: this indicates the existence of a significant process of inclusion of an unemployed labor force and non-remunerated workers into the group of workers who gain an income.
4. This process has been supported by a continuous effort for the improvement of human capital. The level of illiteracy has decreased in the whole nation, but the decrease has been much stronger in Ceara in the last years (2004 compared with 1999), than the NE or Brazil. This improvement is much clearer when we analyze the illiteracy of the youngsters aged 10–14, who are expected to lead the future economic development: the achievement of the CE was as good as in the NE and Brazil for two decades till 1999, but it has been extremely impressive in the first years of the new millennium, much beyond the achievement of the NE and Brazil. The illiteracy rate of these youngsters was always highest in Ceara, today it is much lower than the NE (5.3% compared with 8.0%), and near to closing the gap with Brazil (3.8%). We remember that in the last years of the nineties the illiteracy rate of this group was 2.39 times greater in Ceara than Brazil, and today it is only 1.39 times greater. The result of these efforts is an impressive increase in the average years of schooling in Ceara, at a much higher rate than in the NE or Brazil, providing the basis for greater productivity, higher income levels, and lower poverty rates.
5. Poverty had not decreased in Brazil before the nineties. The diminution of poverty in Brazil happened in the nineties, more or less at similar rates in Ceara, the NE, and Brazil as a whole. Since the beginning of the new millennium, the rate of decrease of poverty has been greater in Ceara than the NE and Brazil, especially in terms of indigent poverty. Moreover, the average income of the poor population increased more rapidly in Ceara during this period, meaning the poor people in Ceara are no longer poorer than the poor people in the NE or Brazil (regarding the indigent poor). We can therefore say that not only has poverty in Ceara decreased in the last few years more rapidly than in other places, but also its profundity is decreasing: fewer poor people, at lower intensity of poverty.

6. All measures of inequality provide signs of impressive improvements achieved by the CE, compared with the NE and Brazil. Inequality has begun some modest decrease only in the nineties, and shows a significant decrease in rates in the new millennium. However, those signs are much clearer and higher in the CE than the NE and Brazil, when measured by any indicator. Gini coefficient decreases more rapidly, the income share of the 50% poorest population increases more rapidly, the income share of the richest 1% decreases more strongly, and the ratio of the income between the 20% richest and 20% poorest population decreases much faster in Ceara than in the NE and Brazil.

The economic growth in the CE and the level of poverty and inequality are still quite high, but the signs shown by a variety of indicators seem to detect a turning point in Ceara in the new millennium – in absolute terms and in comparison with the NE and Brazil. The policy adopted by the CE in the nineties and consolidated in the last few years apparently led to a more appropriate adaptation of the social and demographic structures to the changing economic structures. Better levels of urbanization and employment in the rural area, jointly with improved levels of education, have led to a clear diminution of gaps between the rural and urban area, to higher productivity, lower levels of poverty, lower intensity of poverty, and lower levels of inequality. Even when such improvements happened in the NE and Brazil, the changes detected in Ceara were always much stronger.

A final and important point is that these advances did not restrain the economic growth of the state: on the contrary, during this same period, the economic growth was greater in Ceara than the NE and Brazil.

REFERENCE

IBGE (Instituto Brasileiro de Geografia e Estatistica). (Various years). Pesquisa Nacional por Amostra de Domicilios (PNAD), Ministerio de Planejamento e Orcamento, Rio de Janeiro, Brazil.

CHAPTER 12

CONCLUSION

A process of economic growth can certainly take place with insufficient diminution of poverty and with widening gaps in income distribution. In Ceara, as in many other states in Brazil and in the world, there are problems of poverty and of inequality, besides macroeconomic growth. Although measurement and definition questions may lead to different evaluations of its volume, it is clear that rural poverty is greater than urban poverty in Ceara, and much more than the urban poverty in the Metropolitan Region of Fortaleza. This picture is typical of most states in the process of economic development, and cannot be dismissed as a result of any specific conditions in this state.

The efforts made in most countries in this situation for the stimulation of economic growth are mostly focused on the attraction of industrial and touristic activities, probably with no sufficient regional considerations. Those find the best location in the metropolitan region, where the conditions of access to labor force, the supply of infrastructures, the access to markets, and the touristic resources are best. The urban features that are required for a process of industrialization are much less accessible in the periphery, where cities are much smaller and provide much weaker infrastructures. If we disregard the social inequality problem and the probable future negative implications of unequal distribution on long-term growth, this could theoretically be a steady free market and efficient equilibrium of the core-periphery type, achieved through concentration of the economic activity in the metropolitan region and through increasing inequality in the distribution of income.

Analysis of the changing economic and demographic structures in Ceara raises doubts about the economic efficiency of this solution. Economic growth was actually primarily led by the industrial sector. The share of agriculture in the economy decreases constantly, which is a natural phenomenon in a process of economic development. The continuous relative shrinking of the agricultural economic basis of the rural population imposes hard conditions in the fight against poverty. Rural–urban migration, as problematic as it is in terms of its negative impacts on urban structures, still happens at a lower rate than that of the decrease of the relative weight of agriculture. The public administrators of rural economic development therefore face a situation of continuously decreasing relative resources in relation to the population for which they have to care. The many rural development programs that have been depicted here certainly had a positive contribution toward alleviation of the problem, but the exogenous economic conditions in which they are operating are worsening over time.

The excess labor force from agriculture in the rural area, trying to find employment in non-farm activities, has three options: migrating to the regional town within the Interior, migrating to the metropolitan region, or staying "at home" in the rural area.

1. The growing disproportion that was found in the diagnosis part of this study for year 1999 between the share of the population still staying in the rural area (32%) or the share of labor force in agriculture (40%), and the share of agriculture in total GDP (6%) implies that this is a reaction of despair rather than a healthy efficient response to changing economic conditions. These figures actually imply that about a third of the State population still stays in the rural area and refrains from migrating to urban places because of the lack of job opportunities in the urban area and the long distance from the metropolitan region (Lucas, 2001). In terms of poverty and distribution, if no measures are taken, this population is actually expected to grow poorer in relation to the population that is engaged in more productive activities.
2. The fact that the rural population that is ready to leave the rural area and find alternative non-farm employment, cannot find an appropriate response in the economy of the Interior, is reflected by the high share of migrants having to go to the metropolitan region (60%, as opposed to 40% of the rural migrants who migrate to towns within the Interior). The deficiency of job opportunities is reflected by the rapid growth of employment in services with low and stagnant productivity, again hinting of the existence of disguised unemployment. This again leads to high levels of poverty and inequality.
3. The ability of the metropolitan region to absorb excess labor force is apparently quite restricted: the growth of the industrial sector is not fully reflected by a growth in employment (the share of industry in employment even shows a decreasing trend), and the sector of services grows but shows zero productivity growth. This may indicate that besides the growth of the productive tourism sector, much of the labor force in services actually reflects a growing hidden unemployment in the metropolitan region.

The persistence of poverty and inequality can therefore be explained by a concentration of economic growth in the metropolitan core, while the excess labor force from agriculture cannot find appropriate employment conditions in the rural area or in the local regional towns, or competes mostly for low-productivity jobs in the metropolitan region. The roots of the existence of this persisting poverty and inequality are therefore in the existence of a changing economic structure in the State, which is not met by an appropriately changing demographic structure.

The apparently rational approach of attacking the problem at its source, or fighting poverty where poverty occurs, is not necessarily the more efficient one. Two traditional approaches, one of "compensatory" measures through transfer payments and the other one of focused support to the rural sector where most poverty is concentrated, may be efficient for the alleviation of the symptoms of poverty, but not necessarily adequate for its long-term eradication. Given the results of our analysis showing that poverty and inequality are a consequence of a market failure where structural changes in the economy that are not met by structural adjustments in urbanization and spatial distribution of the population, a focused effort in the solution of pure rural problems may even be counter-productive.

Much research has been done and still needs to be done in order to identify the optimal policy measures to be taken by the government. An approach of "demand-driven" models has been suggested for the specific case of the development of small enterprises in Ceara by Tendler and Amorim (1996), involving the intervention of government as a main purchaser of products. Other approaches require government involvement as a facilitator of development through the provision of appropriate conditions. Supporting the development of a few urban centers within the Interior through building of infrastructures (Bar-El & Benhayoun, 2000), investing in human capital formation, improving public social services, could probably lead to healthier economic growth (Bar-El & Felsenstein, 1990; Epstein & Jezeph, 2001; Isserman, 2001; Kim & Kim, 2002), leading to lower levels of poverty and to a better distribution of income, through the following expected effects:

1. Better conditions in the urban Interior would attract some of the industrial activities, using its potential of abundant supply of land and labor force.
2. Such conditions would attract more rural migrants within the Interior, increasing the urbanization process, and improving the spatial distribution of the population.

3. Diminution of the population in the rural area would improve levels of productivity in agriculture (by diminishing the disguised unemployment) and therefore increase the income level.
4. Stronger urban centers within the Interior can stimulate the development of non-farm employment in the rural sector, by providing necessary economic support services (Biles & Pigozzi, 2000; Zhu, 2000).

The operational conclusion in terms of public policy reached by the Government of Ceara is the need for a combination of sectoral policies (such as support for industry) and regional policies (such as support for infrastructures and education in the Interior) in order to achieve both economic growth and a wider distribution of this growth. Consequently, the following principles of a policy for the promotion of economic development in the Interior are used as basic guidelines:

1. The overall objective is to decrease poverty in the Interior and gaps with RMF, by increasing economic activity.
2. Promoting economic activity in the Interior requires achieving higher levels of competitiveness and of productivity, and an integration of the economy of the Interior into the economy of the State.
3. The State's policy is to achieve that by enabling appropriate external conditions for a healthy development of economic activities within a free market system, by solving regional market failures and bottlenecks.
4. The necessary measures are in terms of restructuring of the spatial distribution of the urban population in the Interior, and facilitating the access of the population to major factors of economic activity (human capital, technology, infrastructures, organizational capacity).
5. Policy measures involve many sectors in the economy and society of the Interior, thus creating a sense of participation and hope.
6. Many policy measures are based on cooperative efforts of various elements in the regions, thus generating the formation of a social capital.
7. Whenever possible, the policy intends to lead to maximum involvement of private-sector business and on local population, with a minimum of direct state intervention.

The solution of the problem of rural poverty therefore requires a comprehensive regional development effort, in which agriculture is an important, but not the only economic resource. A structural change is required in the economy of the Interior, which would enable greater levels of productivity, and consequently lower levels of poverty. The strategy that is elaborated here has already been partly implemented by the government of the State and is therefore oriented toward the achievement of combined targets in three inter-related fields: first is the increase of productivity in the rural sector; second is the increase of non-farm employment supply; third is the stimulation of a continuing process of spatially balanced urbanization.

This "combined strategy" is expected to lead to a sustainable equilibrium in the rural area, stimulating a long-term process of regional development and of diminution of poverty. Each of the three components of this strategy was found unable to solve the problem separately, while there is a synergy effect when using the three components together. Increasing productivity alone would lead to an increasing excess of labor force. Increased productivity does improve competitive ability and therefore the growth of the potential for agricultural and non-agricultural production, but should be complemented by the creation of conditions for the development of new non-farm activities, and by a process of urbanization.

The first component, increasing productivity in the rural sector, is achieved by policy measures that improve the conditions prevailing in that sector. Policy measures for the support of agricultural activities have always been implemented by the government of Ceara, and were supplemented lately by a new program for the development of rural entrepreneurship.

Human capital development by investments in education and professional training is a crucial factor in improving productivity in all economic sectors, and for increasing of employment flexibility. Higher educational and professional levels may play an important role (given other necessary conditions) in the attraction of investments into the Interior. The policy of heavy investment in education has already been implemented and has resulted in significant improvements. However, two aspects of the education policy are deficient and should be reconsidered: firstly the total volume of investments in education is still insufficient, and should be increased in order to lessen the gaps between Ceara and other regions in Brazil; the second and most important aspect is the educational gap between the rural and the urban sectors: this gap has increased over the years (together with the improvement in general educational levels), leading to a relative decrease in the competitive ability of the rural area. It is therefore imperative to take measures with the objective of the diminution of the gaps with other states and the rural–urban gap (increasing total education expenditures, and increasing the share of the rural area). The policy adopted by Ceara in the last years has actually produced positive results in that direction.

Within this first component, we also mentioned the importance of physical as well as social infrastructures. The prevailing policy practice in most countries of the supply of public funds for infrastructures as a response to revealed needs by the population and the economic activity is certainly positive and meets the important requirements of a participative approach. However, as in the case of education, public policy should not only respond to "revealed" demand, but should also secure a normative balanced distribution of its resources for infrastructures in various regions. The government of Ceara has adopted such a budget policy that permits the allocation of appropriate resources for the creation of conditions for increasing productivity and economic growth.

The second component of policy is the stimulation of non-farm activity. The metropolitan region is unable to absorb all the excess labor force from the rural area, and therefore structural changes in the economy of the Interior are needed in addition to the urbanization process. We have shown that the traditional types of non-farm activities in the rural area, such as agro-industries or production for local demand, cannot provide a sufficient response to the increasing employment needs. Most efforts of public policy therefore need to be oriented toward the support of economic activities that have to compete on the external markets. The action which is being taken by the government of Ceara is actually focused on the identification of economic activities that have such a potential, and on the solution of bottlenecks that prevent them from achieving their potential. One of the relevant programs is a monitoring program that assists businesses by enabling them to have access to consultancy, previously almost inaccessible in the conditions of the peripheral regions. The results of the first year of implementation actually show an increased efficiency and access to external markets. Another program that aids in the improvement of access to supporting services that are less accessible in remote regions is the technological improvement program. All these are still in the first stages of implementation, and should be expanded to other regions in the non-metropolitan area.

The third crucial component of public policy is a balanced urbanization process. Spatial urban-restructuring is a major policy strategy for the initiation of a more balanced economic growth, enabling the development of regions outside the metropolitan area, supporting the necessary structural economic changes, and offering the needed backing for the economy of the rural area. The continuing relative growth of the Metropolitan Region of Fortaleza and the parallel relative decrease of the urban population of the Interior may be the most important constraints that are preventing a balanced and healthy growth of the rural area. The State policy, as described in its economic plan, recognizes the existence of this problem, and is considering measures for the "interiorization" of economic development (integration of the non-metropolitan regions into the national economy). It is important to emphasize that "interiorization," as revealed by programs of support to various cities in the Interior, is a necessary but not a sufficient policy. The concept of "concentrated dispersion" has been suggested here, meaning that "interiorization" should be matched with a greater concentration of population within the Interior. In other words, priority should be given to the creation of a few secondary and tertiary cities in the Interior. This is expected to encourage the creation of agglomeration economies, and provide a solid basis for the development of non-farm economic activities in the rural sector. To some extent, such a "spatially balanced urbanization" can be considered as a combination of elements from the "growth pole" theory (Perroux, 1955) and from the secondary cities idea or rural–urban development approach by Rondinelli (1983) and Rondinelli and Ruddle (1978), as presented in more details in the introductory chapter. Efforts in this direction have already been made by the Government of Ceara, with the elaboration of regional development plans for six regions.

The spatial urban-reorganization is complemented by a program of regional economic development units, actually implemented through the establishment of regional offices of the Secretariat of Local and Regional Development. Such offices help in the establishment of Regional Councils in each region, in which the local economic and social leadership is represented, assuring the formation of a social capital in each region, and an active participation of the local population in the process of growth.

A variety of programs that respond to this policy have been implemented by the State of Ceara in some regions. Other programs are still in the stage of assessment or of pilot implementation. The government of Ceara has recently initiated a pilot program of "rural entrepreneurship consultancy." This program aims to increase entrepreneurship and managerial skills among farmers in the rural area, providing them with consultancy services that help them to improve their productivity and to increase the range of their activity. The program is operated by the Secretariat of Agriculture, in coordination with other relevant Secretariats, with the support of the regional offices of the Secretariat of Local and Regional Development, and under the guidance of a government steering committee.

The focus of the program is mainly on the following issues:

- Managerial and marketing consultancy to farmers.
- Development of joint organizations for purchasing raw materials, processing agricultural products, and marketing final products.

- Introduction of technical innovations in agricultural businesses.
- Improving accessibility to financial funds.
- Development of new businesses in agriculture and in non-farm activities.

Another program still in the phase of preliminary examination is a program for the development of technological incubators and for the establishment of technological networks.

The development model in Ceara is based on the evaluation that poverty and inequality are explained by the existence of a basic failure in the adjustment between long-term structural economic changes and spatial demographic changing patterns. The policy derived is therefore one that attempts to eliminate this failure by combining the means for the increase of productivity in the rural area, the solution of bottlenecks in the development of non-farm activities, and a balanced process of urbanization. Such a policy model has been implemented in the State of Ceara for the last few years, and a global evaluation of the results of such a policy should accompany this process. This will require data collection and analysis in the next few years. However, the preliminary results and the intuitive reactions in the field look quite promising in terms of new jobs created, regional cooperation efforts in various economic and social sectors, new relationships between businesses and research institutions, higher levels of participation of the population in the design of the economic and social future of their region, and so on. Such a policy model in Ceara could therefore inspire policy-making in other states and countries that face same problems. As shown in the previous chapters, the evaluation made on the basis of time series of various indicators show quite encouraging signs. In the nineties, Ceara showed quite positive achievements in general, but the most important finding is that since the beginning of the new millennium, the progress made in Ceara is quite clearly much better than the progress made in the Northeast or in Brazil as a whole. This is true for most economic and social indicators: increasing levels of income, decreasing gaps between the rural and urban areas, increasing compatibility between employment and product in agriculture actually leading to higher levels of productivity, decreasing poverty and mainly decreasing indigent poverty, decreasing gaps in level of income of the poor population, etc. Furthermore, besides achieving better results in terms of poverty and inequality reduction in Ceara in comparison with the Northeast and Brazil, the rate of economic growth during the period, since the beginning of the millennium, was on average higher in Ceara.

This leads us to our final note on the question of conflict or complementarity between growth and equality: The achievement of growth with diminution of inequality cannot be considered as an additive process. The model of Ceara as presented here does not advocate the adoption of a policy for maximum growth that would be supplemented by a policy for the diminution of inequality. The message here is that some of the inequality resulting from economic growth may be due to a market failure, and therefore a solution to this failure through public policy may decrease the level of inequality and contribute at the same time to the global growth of the State. It is important to note that such policy is not necessarily the best measure for the achievement of a maximal immediate diminution of inequality. As a first example, the suggested policy of urban-restructuring favors stronger urban places in the periphery, given that the recommended features of such restructuring are expected to provide wide gains to the region as a whole; a second example is the monitoring program: Although it is expected to be applied in poor regions in the periphery, it deals directly with the potential entrepreneurs, who are the stronger elements in the region, and assumes that their actions will engender extended effects. The general idea is therefore to induce economic growth in poor regions, but to focus on the elements with greater potential for growth in those regions (stronger cities, stronger entrepreneurs, etc.), leading to a diminution of gaps between poor and rich regions (but with the potential for an increasing gap within the poor regions). Internal inequalities within the regions would be expected to decrease with the initiation of the process of regional endogenous growth: creation of employment by the new small entrepreneurs, greater demands for agricultural products, greater demand for services, etc. It seems that, after all, the concepts and strategies of growth poles, trickling-down effects, urbanization, and the Kuznets U-curve, may all be actually working, but mostly at the regional level, and after market failures have been taken care of.

REFERENCES

Bar-El, R., & Benhayoun, G. (2000). Convergence, divergence and non-efficiency of public infrastructure spatial allocation. *Région et Developpement*, *12*, 167–181.

Bar-El, R., & Felsenstein, D. (1990). Entrepreneurship and rural industrialization: Comparing patterns of rural and urban locational choice in Israel. *World Development*, *18*(2), 257–267.

Biles, J. J., & Pigozzi, B. W. (2000). The interaction of economic reforms, socio-economic structure and agriculture in Mexico. *Growth and Change*, *31*(1), 3–22.

Epstein, T. S., & Jezeph, D. (2001). Development – there is another way: A rural–urban partnership development paradigm. *World Development*, *29*(8), 1443–1454.

Isserman, A. M. (2001). Competitive advantages of rural America in the next century. *International Regional Science Review*, *24*(1), 38–58.

Kim, E., & Kim, K. (2002). Impacts of regional development strategies on growth and equity of Korea: A multiregional CGE model. *The Annals of Regional Science*, *36*(1), 165–180.

Lucas, R. E. B. (2001). The effects of proximity and transportation on developing country population migrations. *Journal of Economic Geography*, *1*(3), 323–339.

Perroux, F. (1955). Note sur la Notion de Pole de Croissance. *Economie Appliquée*, *8*, 307–320.

Rondinelli, D. A. (1983). *Secondary cities in developing countries: Policies for diffusing urbanization.* New York, NY: Sage Publications.

Rondinelli, D. A., & Ruddle, K. (1978). *Urbanization and rural development: A spatial policy for equitable growth.* New York, NY: Praeger Publishers.

Tendler, J., & Amorim, M. A. (1996). Small firms and their helpers: Lessons on Demand. *World Development*, *24*(3), 407–426.

Zhu, U. (2000). In situ urbanization in rural China: Case studies from Fujian province. *Development and Change*, *31*(2), 413–434.

ABOUT THE AUTHOR

Raphael Bar-El is an economist, Professor at Ben-Gurion University of the Negev and Chair of the Department of Public Policy and Administration. His main areas of interest are: economic growth, regional development, economic cooperation in the Middle East, small towns. In the last few years, he has worked with the State Government of Ceara (Brazil) on policy measures for the alleviation of poverty through economic regional development. He was the Director of the National Economic Planning Authority, at the Ministry of Economy and Planning. He was also a member of the Joint (Jordan–Israel–US) Steering Committee for the Integrated Development of the Jordan Rift Valley (JRV). He was in charge of the Economic Development Plan within the team of the long-term Master Plan for Israel. In 1996 and 1997, he was a member of the project headed by Michael Porter on *Building Regional Competitive Advantage in the Middle East*. Until 1993 he was a researcher and planner, the Director of Research, and finally the Director General of the Development Study Center (DSC), Rehovot, Israel. He has acquired extensive experience in regional development research and planning, in Israeli regions, as well as in regions in the developing world.